CAMBRIAN PERIOD

◀538 - 485 Million Years Ago▶

Vol.1

Designed & Written by
Katya McGuane of Katya's Yarn Bois

ADVANCE PRAISE FOR CROCHET THROUGH THE AGES: CAMBRIAN PERIOD VOL. 1

"Katya has an incredible talent for making unique, well-designed amigurumi patterns. Her work is not only creative for its design, but also for the creatures she chooses to create - she designs lesser-known prehistoric creatures and expertly brings them to life with her hook. There is so much knowledge to uncover here: learning how to advance your crochet skills considerably, and learning about amazing prehistoric creatures along the way!" - Crafty Bean Crochets (@craftybeancrochets)

"Katya's unique patterns are amazingly detailed, with great thought put into shaping and techniques!" - Kristin

"Katya's patterns are truly wonderful. Her passion, talents, and efforts are on full display. What can seem incredibly intimidating, she makes clear and straightforward. Her patterns are fun and full of various techniques. I've loved every single one I've made so far. She's also just a very nice person :)" - Katie (@kozy.ducklings)

"I love the La Brea Tar Pits but hate not being allowed to cuddle the displayed fossils. Thanks to Katya's incredible patterns, I can live my dream and snuggle up with my own ammonite every night!" - Alexis Kavros (@RemyACraftyHedgehog)

"I'm so glad I found Katya's patterns. Being able to work up these bois from her patterns has given me the confidence to design my own patterns and learn new techniques. The sky is the limit. I love that she gives a voice to the voiceless (extinct)" - Cynthia Szamborski (@mama_knot)

"I absolutely love these patterns! I adore each and every detail that goes into each pattern Katya designs. These patterns are so thorough and easy to follow, and make the cutest little creatures too!" - Skylar (@skylarrheacrochet)

"All of Katya's work is amazing and innovative, they are truly unique crochet patterns" - Madison Brown

"The most detailed and fun patterns I've ever seen, absolutely perfect!" - (@crazymousecrochet)

"Katya has some of the best and most unique crochet patterns I have ever seen! They are so detailed that a beginner crocheter could become an advanced one in a matter of hours just by following one of these patterns. Plus, the final products always look stunning!" - DemiRae Lynn (@khaotic_kritters)

CAMBRIAN PERIOD

◄ 538 - 485 MYA ►

A Self-Published Amazon KDP Work by Katya McGuane
Amazon.com, Inc.
410 Terry Avenue North
Seattle, WA 98109-5210
United States
This book is self-published, Amazon claims no association beyond printing this book

First Edition

This book is written using American English language and terminology.

TABLE OF CONTENTS

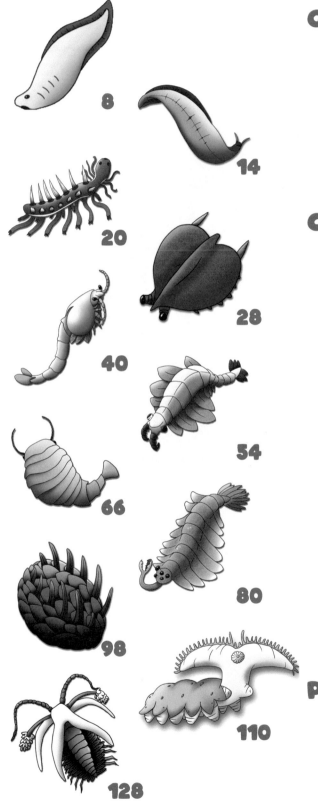

GETTING STARTED

CAMBRIAN CREATURES

POST SCRIPT

v

POST SCRIPT (CONT.)

INTRODUCTION

This book is my love letter to not just the craft of crochet, but to the world of paleontology and all of its goofy critters. I have been crocheting since I was around 8 or 9 when I was first taught by my grandmother (Nannie). Ever since I have been obsessed with the art form. I especially took a liking to amigurumi, as I have always been a big collector of stuffed animals. Once I discovered that I could make my own custom ones, crochet became all I wanted to do! To this day, it is THE thing I love to do with my free time.

My grandmother had taught me the fundamentals of the craft, but I did not know that patterns existed for quite some time. This would actually be a great blessing, as it forced me to get creative and figure out how to design different forms through trial and error, through which I learned the process of crochet pattern design.

In 2020, I had all the time in the world to take my solid foundation of crochet skills to an entirely new level. I finally started to write down my patterns, and over the years I slowly refined that ability as well. At first, I just made some random animals whenever inspiration struck. I grew up with many animal books that are now heavily worn from years of childlike wonder. This early fascination certainly inspired my crochet projects. I had quite a few dinosaur books that got lots of love over the years as well, so I certainly already had an existing interest in the prehistoric.

Everything changed when I was feeling aimless one day. I had decided that I wanted my pattern shop to have a more cohesive theme than simply random animals, so I conducted a poll on my Instagram story (my account didn't even have 100 followers yet). I included four options to vote on, and one of those was prehistoric animals. Prehistoric animals ended up winning 58% of the vote! Part of me somehow knew all along that this was going to end up being my passion, and the vote just confirmed that for me. So I began carving out my niche as a prehistoric animal crochet pattern designer.

But I wanted to do more than just the typical dinosaurs that have already been done well by many talented designers. I wanted to shine a spotlight on the obscure animals that hardly anyone even knows exist. I wasn't sure at first if anyone would even be interested in crocheting animals they've never heard of, but I have never been so happy to be wrong. I have many followers now that absolutely cherish the combined experience of crocheting unique amigurumi and learning about a new piece of prehistory at the same time. I've found that this learning process has made it more enjoyable for me too. I've become somewhat of an amateur paleontology buff since starting this niche.

So I started with some Cambrian animals since it was a non-dinosaur time period I was already familiar with, and I eventually accumulated 11 Cambrian animal designs as I hopped around different eras. This book is the culmination of that beginning of my journey into my life's work as a sort of yarn necromancer of the long extinct creatures that used to call this same Earth home.

I hope you can feel the magic and passion within every page of this book.

MATERIALS & TOOLS:

Crochet Hook

I always use a **2.5 mm crochet hook**, but I tend to crochet a bit on the looser side. If you crochet more tightly, you may find yourself more comfortable using a 3 mm or 4 mm. You just need to make sure that your stuffing does not show through your stitches with whichever hook you end up using.

Worsted (4) Weight Yarn:

My go-to yarn brands are Red Heart and Big Twist because of the color selection, low price, and relatively good size consistency. Red Heart Super Saver can have some thickness variation that you should keep an eye on. Sometimes their skeins can be a bit thicker than usual, but for the most part it's fine. Big Twist is always consistent! But whatever worsted weight yarn you can find in your area should be just fine. (Red Heart and Big Twist are not affiliated with this book whatsoever)

Safety Eyes

Haikouichthys uses one pair of 6 mm safety eyes
Hallucigenia uses one pair of 6 mm safety eyes
Opabinia uses two 12 mm safety eyes and three 8 mm safety eyes
Sidneyia uses one pair of 8 mm safety eyes
Every other pattern uses crocheted eyes

Stem Wire (Also called Floral Wire in some areas)

I recommend the thickest wire you can find. The higher the gauge number, the THINNER the wire. The thickest wire is 8 gauge, and the thinnest is 36. Many of the patterns in this book use it to either make parts of the body poseable, or to add structure and strength to long and thin pieces like antennas.

Darning Needle

I recommend bent tip darning needles (also called yarn needles) for amigurumi; it makes it easier to sew pieces together in three dimensions.

Recommended: Stitch Markers

I highly advise using stitch markers so that you don't lose your place in your rounds. The alignment of the beginning of your rounds is very important for the overall construction of your piece.

Recommended: Sewing Pins

Sewing pins are very helpful for pinning pieces into place to make sewing easier. Having pieces secured ahead of time will reduce the amount of trial and error you have to do when sewing pieces on.

TERMINOLOGY:

Not all of these terms will be used in this book, this is to serve as a master list of terms.

[_____] __x	These brackets indicate that the series of stitches within them will be repeated as many times as is noted after the brackets. For example, [sc 1, inc] 6x means to sc 1, then increase, and repeat this sequence 6 times.
{_____}	Every stitch noted between these brackets is done in the same stitch
(____ st)	Indicates how many stitches will be in the finished row/round
(____ rows)	Indicates how many rows are in a series of rows
(____ rounds)	Indicates how many rounds are in a series of rounds.
2/3 Dec	Make one decrease, then make a second decrease, but make the first stitch of this second decrease start in the same stitch where your first decrease ended. This is used when going from an odd number of stitches to an even number and is used to maintain symmetry.
2/3 Inc	Make a single crochet, then you will make a decrease starting in the stitch that you just made a sc into and ending in the stitch after it. After the decrease, sc one more time in the same stitch that your decrease just ended in. This is used as an increase when going from an even number to an odd number so that it can be made in the center of the row to maintain symmetry.
BLO	Back Loops Only
Bob St	Bobble Stitch
Bpsc	Back Post Single Crochet
Ch	Chain
Cont.	Continue/continued
Dc	Double Crochet
Dc Dec	Double Crochet Decrease (yarn over and insert into first stitch, pull up a loop, yarn over and pull through two loops, then yarn over and insert into second stitch, pull up a loop, yarn over and pull through two loops, then yarn over and pull through last two loops)
Dc Inc	Double Crochet Increase (two double crochets in one stitch)
Dec	Decrease (single crochet 2 stitches together)
Ddsc	Drop Down Single Crochet: When working in a row that has slip stitches, instead of single crocheting into the top of that slip stitch, you will 'drop down' and single crochet in the sc stitch below that slst (the stitch that the slst itself was worked into), encasing the slip stitch(es) above. If you are following two rounds of slip stitches, then you will drop down to the sc stitch two rounds down. This will create a curling effect over time. The rule of thumb is that you will never be working into any of the slip stitches with this technique, it should always be a sc stitch no matter how far down it is.

Ddslst	Drop Down Slip Stitch: When you are making more than one slst row before a ddsc row, your 2nd, 3rd, 4th, etc slst stitches will all go into the last sc stitch that lies underneath the slst(s) from previous round(s), encasing the slip stitch(es) above. As with the ddsc on page 3, the rule of thumb is that you will never work into a slip stitch with this technique, it should always be a sc stitch no matter how far down it is. It will get tight with more and more rounds of ddslst.
Fpsc	Front Post Single Crochet
FLO	Front Loops Only
Hdc	Half Double Crochet
Hdc Dec	Half Double Crochet Decrease: Yarn over and insert into first stitch and pull up loop. Then, yarn over and insert into the next stitch and pull up a loop. Yarn over and pull through all loops.
Hdc Inc	Half Double Crochet Increase (two half double crochets in one stitch)
Inc	Increase (2 sc in one stitch)
Invisible Join	Involves slst joining to the first stitch of the round and chaining one, but you will take the hook out of the loop and pull it through the back. Scan this QR code for a more thorough tutorial. *ALWAYS begin a joined round in the SAME stitch that you joined to, NOT the one after it* https://www.youtube.com/shorts/wFn6YYkBmWY
Round	Indicates that you will be working in a round
Row	Indicates that you will chain and turn your work (working in rows)
Sc	Single Crochet
Slst	Slip Stitch
St	Stitch
Trc	Treble Crochet (Triple Crochet)
Trp Inc	Triple Increase (3 sc in one stitch)
Trp Dec	Triple Decrease (sc 3 together)

SEWING TECHNIQUES:

WHIP STITCH

Sew in a loopedy-loop motion, meaning that you will always be inserting your needle on the same side every time. This will help blend the two pieces together to create a more seamless look, and it works best when both pieces are the same yarn color.

INVISIBLE STITCH

Don't work directly on the edge of the work. Instead, insert the needle through both layers as shown to the right and sew in this manner. This helps to preserve the depth of the layers and also to keep the edges clean when sewing with two different yarn colors.

ZIGZAG STITCH

Sew from side A to side B, then back through the next stitch on side B and back to side A again, working in a zigzag manner. This technique is functionally similar to the invisible stitch, except you work through the edges of your work instead of offset from the edge. This can help give you an invisible seam in some contexts. I generally use it to close off seams that are lines rather than circles.

SEAMLESS STITCH

This technique is particularly helpful when joining two different colored pieces, so the instructions will be told in terms of working with two colors. Choose one color as your base to work from (Color A). Insert your needle through Color A, then exit through Color B (Fig. 1). Then, loop around the stitch of Color B (Fig. 2) and reinsert into the same stitch from Color A (Fig. 3). Repeat this sequence all the way around.

For the smoothest join, finish off the stitch in Fig. 3 by working only in the front loop of the stitch. To be clear, the Fig. 1 step is worked in both loops, and Fig. 3 is finished off in the front loop only.

FIGURE 1

FIGURE 2

FIGURE 3

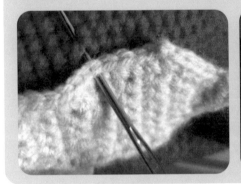

THE CAMBRIAN PERIOD
..... 538-485 Million Years Ago ....

The Cambrian Period of Earth's history is regarded as the moment where animal life really began to kick off, earning itself the nickname "The Cambrian Explosion". It was also the first time that we know of that animals began to prey on other animals, which caused evolution to accelerate.

Fossils from this era were first discovered in the Burgess Shale formation in the Canadian Rockies of British Columbia by paleontologist Charles Walcott in 1909. The first creature he identified from the rock was Sidneyia, which he named after his son Sidney. Marrella was so common in these deposits that it has its own layer named after it! Over the next 18 years, Walcott would collect around 65,000 individual specimens from this formation, dedicating his life to describing them all.

During the Cambrian Period, the earth's landscape was very different from what we know today. Most of the land was crammed together in the southern hemisphere of the planet in a supercontinent called Pannotia, which was slowly breaking apart into separate land masses throughout the Cambrian. There was no sea ice at the time, so the sea levels were quite high. This provided sea creatures with the warm, shallow environments they needed to thrive.

At this time, there was no life on the surface of the land other than mats of microbes on the coasts. Complex life was limited to the oceans for now, and these oceans were dominated by the arthropods (invertebrates with exoskeletons). Anomalocaris was the apex predator at this time, measuring around 1.5-3 ft long and preying on just about any soft-bodied creature that was unlucky enough to cross its path. It used its state of the art compound eyes to get around, a structure that is believed to have evolved during the Cambrian.

In order to avoid the grasp of predators like Anomalocaris, prey animals had to evolve defensive structures. Hallucigenia evolved long spines on its back, Trilobites developed hard shells, and Wiwaxia had a mixture of both! This was a time of immense diversity of form for both predator and prey.

Arthropods weren't the only creatures swimming around in Cambrian waters; the ancestors of all vertebrates were out there, lying low to avoid the arthropod beasts. At this time, their spinal cords were not protected by bones, giving them the name *Chordate* instead of *Vertebrate*. Pikaia and Haikouichthys were both part of this phylum!

The Cambrian came to an end 485 million years ago with the Cambrian-Ordovician Extinction Event, which is believed to have been caused by volcanic activity as well as sea level and oxygen changes, leading to a mass die-off of the life forms that called this time period home.

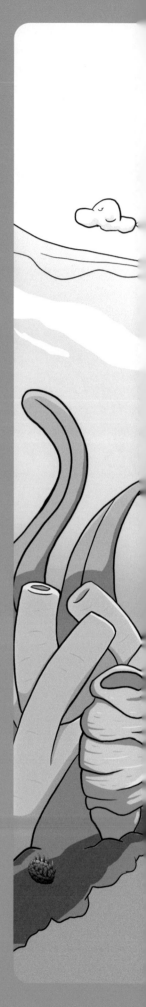

HAIKOUICHTHYS
(High-koo-ICK-theez)

MATERIALS

2.5 mm Crochet Hook (or hook size of your choice)
Yarn (All Worsted Weight):

Body Color	Less than 1/4 of a 364 yd skein
Fin Color	Only a few yards
Gill Color	Only a few yards

Stuffing
One Pair of 6 mm Safety Eyes
Darning Needle
Stitch Marker
Sewing Pins

WHAT WAS HAIKOUICHTHYS?

Haikouichthys was one of the earliest fish species on Earth! Though some scientist prefer to refer to it as a proto-fish rather than a true fish. Before its discovery, fish were believed to have evolved 50 million years later. Though likely not our direct ancestor, Haikouichthys gave rise to the vertebrate phylum that would eventually contain the human species!

It was much smaller than the one you're about to crochet, measuring around 1 inch (2.5 cm) long. It was a chordate, meaning it had a spinal cord but no spinal bones to protect it. It also lacked a jaw (jaws would not evolve in vertebrates until the Silurian period 430 MYA!)

One might be inclined to believe that it was named after the Japanese style of poetry, the Haiku, but it was actually found in Haikou, an area in Kunming City, Yunnan Province, China. Its full name means "Fish from Haikou".

The body and head were two separate segments and it had 6-9 gill slits on each side of its body. On the underside of its body, it had 13 circular structures, which some scientists speculate may have been sexual organs.

Since it was soft and fleshy, it was more maneuverable than arthropods like Anomalocaris. And due to its lack of a jaw, it likely scavenged flesh from injured or dead animals rather than actively hunting.

DIFFICULTY:

BEGINNER

BODY

Use **body color** yarn. Stuff the whole piece as you go along.

Round 1	Ch 2, sc 6 in 2nd ch from hook (6 st)
Round 2	Sc 6 (6 st)
Round 3	Inc 3, sc 3 (9 st)
Round 4	Sc 9 (9 st)
Round 5	[Sc 1, inc] 3x, sc 3 (12 st)
Round 6	Sc 12 (12 st)
Round 7	[Sc 1, inc] 6x (18 st)
Round 8-9	Sc 18 (18 st per round) (2 rounds)
Round 10	[Sc 2, inc] 6x (24 st)

Round 11-20	Sc 24 (24 st per round) (10 rounds)
Round 21	[Sc 6, dec] 3x (21 st)
Round 22-24	Sc 21 (21 st per round) (3 rounds)
Round 25	[Sc 5, dec] 3x (18 st)
Round 26-28	Sc 18 (18 st per round) (3 rounds)
Round 29	[Sc 4, dec] 3x (15 st)
Round 30-32	Sc 15 (15 st per round) (3 rounds)
Round 33	[Sc 3, dec] 3x (12 st)
Round 34-36	Sc 12 (12 st per round) (3 rounds)
Round 37	[Sc 2, dec] 3x (9 st)
Round 38-40	Sc 9 (9 st per round) (3 rounds)
Round 41	[Sc 1, dec] 3x (6 st)
Finishing Off	After finishing this round, slst to next st, cut and tie off, sew remaining hole closed, weave in end

Adding Safety Eyes

Fold the piece in half so that the side with the 3 increases from Round 3 are on the bottom, as shown below. Place the eyes between Rounds 3 and 4 with about 2 stitches of space between them across the top. The ends of the safety eyes will probably be tight in the tip of the nose, but it should fit just fine.

END RESULT

BACK FIN

Use **fin color** yarn.

Row 1	Ch 41, starting in 2nd ch from hook: slst 2, sc 10, inc, trp inc, inc, sc 10, hdc 5, dc 4, hdc 2, sc 2, slst (43 st)
Finishing Off	Cut and tie off, leaving long tail for sewing.

END RESULT

ATTACHING BACK FIN TO BODY

Alignment	Place the fin so that the corner curves around the tail tip of the body, as shown to the right. Make sure the fin goes along the top and bottom of the body, with the longer side on the top of the body, centered between the eyes. I recommend holding it in place with sewing pins.
Sewing	Use <u>whip stitch sewing technique</u> to secure the fin to the body.

EMBROIDERING GILLS

Gill Placement	Cut a piece of **gill color** yarn. Embroider about 6 short vertical lines on each side of the fish, starting about 5 rounds back from the eyes.

FINAL PRODUCT

Your Haikouichthys is officially complete! Check back with the photo on page 11 to make sure that your piece looks as intended.

PIKAIA
(Pih-KYE-uh)

MATERIALS

2.5 mm Crochet Hook (or hook size of your choice)
Yarn (All Worsted Weight):

Body Color	Less than 1/2 of a 364 yd skein
Fin & Leg Color	Only a few yards

Stuffing
Stem Wire
Darning Needle
Stitch Marker
Sewing Pins

WHAT WAS PIKAIA?

Pikaia was an early chordate (meaning it had a spinal chord, but not necessarily a bony spine). These little guys were quite small, only measuring around 1.5-2 inches (3-5 cm) long!

It was discovered by Charles Walcott in the famous Cambrian fossil deposit, the Burgess Shale in British Columbia. Pikaia's name comes from the Pika Peak mountain in Alberta, Canada. Walcott initially described Pikaia as belonging to the annelid phylum, which includes segmented worms like today's modern earthworms. But as of now, they are simply placed into their own family within the chordate group. However, even this position is contested. It is extremely difficult to classify ancient fossilized remains!

The Pikaia was an ocean-dwelling creature that likely swam like modern day eels, and it was probably a filter feeder that fed on small food particles in the water. For a while, Pikaia was believed to have been the ultimate grandfather to all vertebrate life including humans, but upon further analysis, it would seem that Pikaia was merely a relative and not the direct ancestor itself. There were also theories that Pikaia was the first ever fish, but this has also proven to be an inaccurate assessment.

Pikaia's body was covered with a cuticle, which is a strong but flexible covering that protected the animal from predators while still allowing it the flexibility to move fluidly. This structure is typically found in invertebrates, which highlights Pikaia's limbo position between the historical arthropod dominance and the rise of the chordates and eventually vertebrates.

Finished Size:
Approx. 11 in
(28 cm) long
from head to
tail. Results may
vary depending on
individual tension.

DIFFICULTY:

ADVANCED BEGINNER

BODY

Use **body color** yarn. You will be working the piece from tail to head, follow stuffing instructions throughout the pattern.

Round 1	Ch 2, sc 6 in 2nd ch from hook (6 st)
Important Technique Note	From this point onward, you will work everything in the **Front Loops Only** for two reasons: to prevent the rounds from shifting and twisting your increases over time, and to make the upcoming surface crochet parts much easier to keep straight.
Round 2	[Sc 2, inc] 2x (8 st)
Round 3	[Sc 3, inc] 2x (10 st)
Round 4	[Sc 4, inc] 2x (12 st)
Round 5	[Sc 5, inc] 2x (14 st)
Round 6	[Sc 6, inc] 2x (16 st)
Round 7	[Sc 7, inc] 2x (18 st)
Round 8	[Sc 8, inc] 2x (20 st)
Round 9	[Sc 9, inc] 2x (22 st)
Round 10	[Sc 10, inc] 2x (24 st)
Round 11	[Sc 11, inc] 2x (26 st)
Round 12	[Sc 12, inc] 2x (28 st)
Round 13	[Sc 13, inc] 2x (30 st)
Round 14	[Sc 14, inc] 2x (32 st)
Round 15	[Sc 15, inc] 2x (34 st)
Round 16	[Sc 16, inc] 2x (36 st)
Round 17-36	Sc 36 (36 st per round) (20 rounds)
Round 37	Sc 14, dec, sc 16, dec, sc 2 (34 st)
Round 38	Sc 34 (34 st)
Round 39	Sc 13, dec, sc 15, dec, sc 2 (32 st)
Round 40	Sc 32 (32 st)
Round 41	Sc 12, dec, sc 14, dec, sc 2 (30 st)

Stem Wire & Stuffing Note	Cut a long length of stem wire and bend it so that it follows the shape of the tip of the tail. Make sure that you have at least four inches (10 cm) of excess sticking out beyond the edge of Round 40 (you can always trim excess later). Insert the stem wire so that it lines the edges of the shape when sitting flat. Then stuff around it.

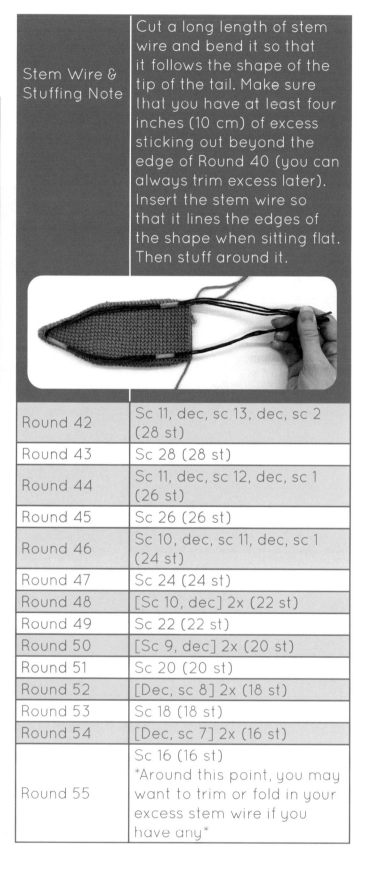

Round 42	Sc 11, dec, sc 13, dec, sc 2 (28 st)
Round 43	Sc 28 (28 st)
Round 44	Sc 11, dec, sc 12, dec, sc 1 (26 st)
Round 45	Sc 26 (26 st)
Round 46	Sc 10, dec, sc 11, dec, sc 1 (24 st)
Round 47	Sc 24 (24 st)
Round 48	[Sc 10, dec] 2x (22 st)
Round 49	Sc 22 (22 st)
Round 50	[Sc 9, dec] 2x (20 st)
Round 51	Sc 20 (20 st)
Round 52	[Dec, sc 8] 2x (18 st)
Round 53	Sc 18 (18 st)
Round 54	[Dec, sc 7] 2x (16 st)
Round 55	Sc 16 (16 st) *Around this point, you may want to trim or fold in your excess stem wire if you have any*

Round 56	[Dec, sc 6] 2x (14 st)
Round 57	Sc 14 (14 st)
Round 58	[Dec, sc 5] 2x (12 st)
Round 59	Sc 12 (12 st)
Round 60	Sc 1, inc 3, sc 3, inc 3, sc 2 (18 st)
Round 61	Sc 18 (18 st)
Round 62	Sc 4, ch 5, starting in 2nd ch from hook: slst 4, continue in next st of round: sc 6, ch 5, starting in 2nd ch from hook: slst 4, continue in next st of round: sc 8 (18 st and 2 antenna pieces)
Round 63	Dec 2, skip around the first antenna (making sure the antennae are on the outside of your work), dec, sc 2, dec, skip around the second antenna, dec 2, sc 4 (12 st)
Finishing Off	Slst to next st, cut and tie off, stuff if needed, sew the remaining hole closed in a horizontal line using whip stitch sewing technique in the front loops only, weave in end.

END RESULT

BACK FIN

Use **fin & leg color** yarn. You will be attaching your yarn to the body and surface crocheting.

Attaching Yarn	Flatten the body as much as possible along the edge where the increases and decreases were made in the body. Then, count up to Round 26 of the body and attach your yarn to the post of the stitch that is perfectly centered along the flat edge of the body. You will be making your first stitch into this stitch.
Row 1	Ch 1, starting in the same stitch you just attached your yarn to (working down towards the tail putting 1 stitch in the side of each round): sc 2, hdc 2, dc 12, hdc 5, sc 5, trp inc in the tip of the tail, continue back up the other side: sc 5, hdc 5, dc 12, hdc 2, sc 2, turn without chaining (55 st)
Row 2	Skip first stitch, sc 1, hdc 2, dc 12, hdc 5, sc 6, trp inc, sc 6, hdc 5, dc 12, hdc 2, sc 2, slst to the next available stitch of the surface of the body (57 st)
Finishing Off	Cut and tie off, weave in ends.

END RESULT

Row 2	Starting in the 2nd ch from hook: slst 3, return to next stitch of row: sc 1, [ch 4, starting in 2nd ch from hook: slst 3, return to the next stitch of row: sc 1] 7x, slst to next available stitch of the surface of the body (8 st, 8 legs)
Finishing Off	Cut and tie off, weave in all ends.

LEGS (REPEAT 2X)

Use **fin & leg color** yarn. You will be attaching your yarn to the body and surface crocheting.

Attaching Yarn	You will attach your yarn to Round 50 of the body. The two leg pieces should be 6 stitches apart from each other along the bottom of the body, so center them so that this 6 stitch-wide space is centered with the head. The stitch markers show exactly where to attach your yarn. You will make your first stitch in the same stitch where you attached your yarn.
Row 1	Surface crochet up the neck: sc 8, ch 4 and turn (8 st)

END RESULT

FINAL PRODUCT

Your Pikaia is officially complete! Check out the gallery to the right to make sure your piece came out as intended.

HALLUCIGENIA
(Huh-LOO-sih-JEN-ee-uh)

MATERIALS

2.5 mm Crochet Hook (or hook size of your choice)
Yarn (All Worsted Weight):

Leg & Side Color	Less than 1/2 of a 364 yd skein
Stomach Color	Less than 1/2 of a 364 yd skein
Back Color	Less than 1/2 of a 364 yd skein
Spine Color	Less than 1/4 of a 364 yd skein
Mouth Color	Only a few yards

Stuffing
One Pair of 6 mm Safety Eyes
Stem Wire (The strongest you can find)
Darning Needle
Stitch Marker
Sewing Pins

WHAT WAS HALLUCIGENIA?

Hallucigenia was by far one of the strangest creatures of the Cambrian Period. Its name stems from "hallucinogen", because it looks like something you would see while hallucinating!

It was a "lobopod", which is a phylum that includes worm-like marine creatures. Though this crochet pattern is quite large, the real Hallucigenia was only around 3/16 to 2 3/16 in (0.5-5.5 cm) long. It had 7 pairs of spines on its back and 7 or 8 pairs of legs.

When it was first discovered, scientists were looking at it upside down! Its legs were believed to be tentacles on its back, while its back spines were thought to be its legs. It is now understood that the spines were defensive structures that protected it from predators that may swoop down to eat it.

When placed under an electron microscope, scientists discovered that Hallucigenia had a small pair of eyes and a mouth full of sharp teeth. It's not clear what it ate, but its mouth structure seems to imply that it would suck food into its mouth, somehow using the ring of teeth to do so.

It's also possible that its legs were not sturdy enough to stand, but were instead used to cling to its environment. They had two claws on the end of each foot that may have aided in this maneuver.

Fun fact: There is a Hallucigenia in Attack on Titan!

Finished Size:
Approx. 12 in
(30 cm) long
from head to tail,
and 8 inches (20 cm)
tall. Results may
vary depending on
individual tension.

DIFFICULTY:

INTERMEDIATE

HEAD & BODY

Start with <u>mouth color</u> yarn. You will switch between mouth, back, leg/side, and stomach color yarn when prompted. The colors will be notated as follows:

M = Mouth
B = Back
L = Leg/Side
S = Stomach

You can use <u>fair isle</u> or <u>intarsia</u> color changing techniques for this piece.

Round 1	Ch 2, sc 6 in 2nd ch from hook (6 st)
Color Change & Technique Note	Switch to **stomach color** yarn. From this point on, work everything in **FLO** to keep your color work straight.
Round 2	S: Inc 6 (12 st)
Round 3	S: [Sc 1, inc] 6x (18 st)
Round 4-5	S: Sc 18 (18 st per round) (2 rounds)
Round 6	L: Slst, sc 5, S: sc 12 (18 st) *Starting the round with a slst will make the color transition smoother*
Round 7-9	L: Sc 6, S: sc 12 (18 st per round) (3 rounds)
Adding Safety Eyes	Place the safety eyes between Rows 7 and 8 on the edges of the pink, as shown below.
Round 10	L: Sc 4, dec, S: [sc 4, dec] 2x (15 st)

Round 11-15	L: Sc 5, S: sc 10 (15 st per round) (5 rounds)
Stem Wire	Cut a length of stem wire that is around 15" (38 cm) long. Fold the end over on itself to round out the end of the wire to prevent poke-through. Insert the stem wire into the head and stuff around it. You will keep stuffing it as you go.
Round 16	L: Sc 3, dec, S: [sc 3, dec] 2x (12 st)
Round 17-29	L: Sc 4, S: sc 8 (12 st per round) (13 rounds)
Round 30	L: [Sc 1, inc] 2x, S: [sc 1, inc] 4x (18 st)
Round 31	L: [Sc 2, inc] 2x, S: [sc 2, inc] 4x (24 st)
Round 32	L: Sc 3, B: sc 2, L: sc 3, S: sc 15 (23 st, 24 st total in round) *This round will stop one stitch short of a full round to shift alignment, move stitch marker accordingly (shift your marker every time you see this note)*
Round 33	L: Sc 3, B: sc 4, L: sc 3, S: sc 14 (24 st)
Round 34	L: Sc 2, B: sc 6, L: sc 2, S: sc 13 (23 st, 24 st total in round) *This round will stop one stitch short of a full round*

Round 35	L: Sc 2, B: sc 8, L: sc 2, S: sc 12 (24 st)
Round 36	L: Sc 2, B: sc 8, L: sc 2, S: sc 11 (23 st, 24 st total in round) *This round will stop one stitch short of a full round*
Round 37	L: Sc 2, B: sc 10, L: sc 2, S: sc 10 (24 st)
Round 38	L: Sc 2, B: sc 10, L: sc 2, S: sc 9 (23 st, 24 st total in round) *This round will stop one stitch short of a full round*
Round 39-65	L: Sc 2, B: sc 12, L: sc 2, S: sc 8 (24 st per round) (27 rounds)
Round 66	L: Sc 2, dec, B: [sc 2, dec] 2x, L: dec, sc 2, S: [sc 2, dec] 2x (18 st)
Round 67	S: Sc 1, L: sc 3, B: sc 4, L: sc 3, S: sc 7 (18 st)
Round 68	S: Sc 3, L: sc 6, S: sc 9 (18 st) *Bend the end of your stem wire in so that it will fit in the end of the body*
Round 69	S: [Sc 1, dec] 6x (12 st)
Round 70	S: Dec 6 (6 st)
Finishing Off	Cut and tie off, sew remaining hole closed, weave in end. You may need to give the piece a little twist to get the color work to sit straight.

END RESULT

LEGS (MAKE 14)

Start with **back color** yarn. You will switch to **leg/side color** when prompted. Lightly stuff the piece so that you can still insert stem wire later on.

Round 1	Ch 2, sc 6 in 2nd ch from hook (6 st)
Round 2	[Sc 1, inc] 3x, (9 st)
Round 3-4	Sc 9 (9 st per round) (2 rounds)
Color Change	Switch to **leg/side color** yarn.
Round 5	Slst, sc 8 (9 st)
Round 6-20	Sc 9 (9 st per round) (15 rounds)
*Row 21-22	Sc 6, ch 1 and turn (6 st per row) (2 rows)
*Round 23	[Sc 1, dec] 2x, work in the side of the rows: sc 1, drop down to unworked stitches in round below: sc 3, work up the side of the rows: sc 1, slst to first stitch of this round (9 st)
Finishing Off	Cut and tie off, leaving long tail for sewing. Bend the end of a piece of stem wire over itself to prevent poke-through and insert into the leg. Cut the stem wire so that there is about half an inch of excess poking out of the opening. I recommend wrapping the exposed tip tightly with Scotch tape to make later insertion easier.

END RESULT

ATTACHING LEGS

Alignment	Place 7 legs on each side of the body, making sure that the taller side (Row 21-23 piece) of the leg is facing outward from the body. The body of the Hallucigenia begins where the piece expands to 24 stitches around. The skinnier part will be the head and neck and will not have any of these legs attached to it.

When placing the legs on, you will push the piece of stem wire that is sticking out from your legs into the body by pushing it into a stitch. By having some of the stem wire inside of the body, you will stabilize the limbs and secure the joint between the leg and body. |
| Alignment cont. | To make sure your spacing is even, I recommend testing out the spacing before sewing by placing all of the legs on without sewing. Start by sewing on the frontmost and backmost sets of legs, then the middle set of legs. The remaining four pairs of legs will be easier to space out evenly. |
| Sewing | Use seamless sewing technique. |

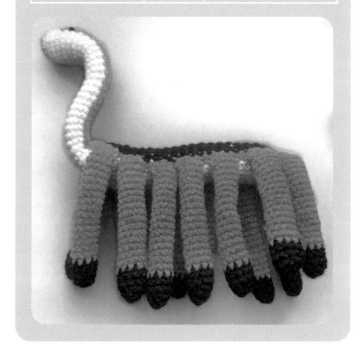

BACK SPINES (MAKE 14)

Start with **spine color** yarn. You will switch to **mouth color** and finally **back color** when prompted to do so. No need to stuff these pieces.

Round 1	Ch 2, sc 4 in 2nd ch from hook (4 st)
Round 2-6	Sc 4 (4 st per round) (5 rounds)
Round 7	Sc 3, inc (5 st)
Round 8-13	Sc 5 (5 st per round) (6 rounds)
Round 14	Sc 4, inc (6 st)
Round 15-19	Sc 6 (6 st per round) (5 rounds)
Color Change	Switch to **mouth color** yarn.
Round 20	Slst, sc 5 (6 st)
Round 21-23	Sc 6 (6 st per round) (3 rounds)
Color Change	Switch to **back color** yarn.
Round 24	Inc 6 (12 st)
Round 25	Sc 12 (12 st)
Finishing Off & Adding Stem Wire	Slst to next st, cut and tie off, leaving long tail for sewing. Then, bend the end of a piece of stem wire over itself to prevent poke-through and insert into the spine. Cut the stem wire so that there is about half an inch of excess poking out of the opening. I recommend tightly wrapping the end in Scotch tape to make later insertion easier

END RESULT

ATTACHING SPINES

Alignment	Place 7 spines on each side of the back in line with all of the legs. Just like with the legs, push the exposed stem wire end into the inside of the body to stabilize the joint between the spines and body. The spines will point outwards rather than straight upwards.
Sewing	Use <u>seamless sewing technique</u>.

NECK APPENDAGES (MAKE 6)

Use **leg/side color** yarn.

Row 1	Ch 11, starting in 2nd ch from hook: [sc 2, inc] 3x, sc 1 (13 st)
Finishing Off	Cut and tie off, leaving long tail for sewing

END RESULT

ATTACHING NECK APPENDAGES

Alignment	Place three appendages on each side of the neck along the pink and white edge, as shown below.
Sewing	Use whip stitch sewing technique to sew one end of each piece on.

FINAL PRODUCT

Your Hallucigenia is officially complete! Check out the gallery to the right to make sure your piece came out as intended.

DUPLAPEX
(DOO-pluh-pex)

MATERIALS

2.5 mm Crochet Hook (or hook size of your choice)
Yarn (All Worsted Weight):

Main Color	About 1/2 of a 364 yd skein
Body Color	Less than 1/2 of a 364 yd skein
Tail Color	Less than 1/4 of a 364 yd skein
Eye Color	Only a few yards

Stuffing
Darning Needle
Stitch Marker
Sewing Pins

WHAT WAS DUPLAPEX?

Unfortunately, very little is known about Duplapex. In fact, it is so obscure that if you try looking up "Duplapex", most of the results will be for "duplex homes". In order to get the right results, you may have to search "Duplapex -duplex" to filter out the houses! And even then, you will only find a handful of photos, some of them being my own artwork!

As of writing this page, there are only two scholarly articles that even mention this creature, one of which is hidden behind a hefty paywall, and the other only briefly mentions its name a handful of times.

What we do know is that Duplapex is an offshoot species from the Tuzoia genus, a shrimp-like arthropod with a big saddle-shaped shell on its back. Tuzoia was around 9 inches (23 cm) long, so it's likely that Duplapex was a similar size

as well, making your project just about life-sized! Another key difference is that Tuzoia had a shovel-shaped tail, while Duplapex had the two pointed spines on either side of the back of its shell. Both had very similar eye stalks and leg compositions.

Tuzoia (and likely also Duplapex) was an active swimmer, but its soft tissues suggest that it "swam close to the seafloor [...] as a predator or a scavenger". This habit of staying close to the ocean floor is called "nektobenthic"! It may have also been able to walk around on the ground, and since Duplapex did not have the same paddle tail as Tuzoia, it may have been more of a scuttler.

This project might just be the rarest creature you ever crochet! And it makes a great Valentine's Day gift to the paleontology lover in your life due to its heart shape!

Finished Size:
Approx. 10 in
(25 cm) long
from head to tail,
and 7 inches (18 cm)
wide. Results may
vary depending on
individual tension.

DIFFICULTY:

INTERMEDIATE

SHELL

Use **main color** yarn. You will start by making three small separate pieces, then you will crochet them all together into a single round. You will very lightly stuff this piece to give it some body, but do not over-stuff it. You will want it to be able to lay pretty flat.

Piece 1	
Round 1	Ch 6, starting in the 2nd ch from hook: sc 4, inc, continue along the bottom of your work starting in the bottom of the inc stitch: sc 4, inc (12 st)
Round 2	Inc, sc 3, inc 3, sc 3, inc 2 (18 st)
Round 3	Sc 18 (18 st)
Round 4	Sc 1, inc, sc 3, [sc 1, inc] 3x, sc 3, [sc 1, inc] 2x (24 st)
Round 5	Sc 24 (24 st)
Round 6	Sc 2, inc, sc 3, [sc 2, inc] 3x, sc 3, [sc 2, inc] 2x (30 st)
Finishing Off	Cut and tie off, weave in end.

Piece 2	
Round 1	Ch 2, sc 4 in 2nd ch from hook (4 st)
Round 2	[Sc 1, inc] 2x (6 st)
Round 3	Sc 6 (6 st)
Round 4	[Sc 1, inc] 3x (9 st)
Round 5	Sc 9 (9 st)
Round 6	[Sc 2, inc] 3x (12 st)
Finishing Off	Cut and tie off, weave in end.

END RESULT

END RESULT

Piece 3	
Round 1	Ch 6, starting in the 2nd ch from hook: sc 4, inc, continue along the bottom of your work starting in the bottom of the inc stitch: sc 4, inc (12 st)
Round 2	Inc, sc 3, inc 3, sc 3, inc 2 (18 st)
Round 3	Sc 18 (18 st)
Round 4	Sc 1, inc, sc 3, [sc 1, inc] 3x, sc 3, [sc 1, inc] 2x (24 st)
Round 5	Sc 24 (24 st)
Round 6	Sc 2, inc, sc 3, [sc 2, inc] 3x, sc 3, [sc 2, inc] 2x (30 st)

Round 7 (Joining Round)	Sc 15, grab Piece 2 and begin working in its first available stitch: sc 6, grab Piece 1 and begin working in its first available stitch: sc 30, continue in the next available stitch of Piece 2: sc 6, continue in the next available stitch of Piece 3: sc 13 (70 st, 72 st total in round) *This round stops 2 st short of a full round to shift the alignment of the first stitch of your round*
Check-In	

Round 8	[Inc 3, sc 33] 2x (78 st)
Round 9	[Sc 1, inc] 3x, sc 33, [sc 1, inc] 3x, sc 33 (84 st)
Round 10	[Sc 2, inc] 3x, sc 33, [sc 2, inc] 3x, sc 33 (90 st)
Round 11-25	Sc 90 (90 st per round) (15 rounds)
Round 26	Sc 7, dec 3, sc 39, dec 3, sc 32 (84 st)
Round 27-29	Sc 84 (84 st per round) (3 rounds)
Round 30	Sc 7, dec 3, sc 36, dec 3, sc 29 (78 st)
Round 31-32	Sc 78 (78 st per round) (2 rounds)
Round 33	Sc 6, dec 3, sc 33, dec 3, sc 27 (72 st)
Round 34	Sc 72 (72 st)
Round 35	Sc 5, dec 3, sc 30, dec 3, sc 25 (66 st)
Round 36	Sc 66 (66 st)
Round 37	Sc 4, dec 3, sc 27, dec 3, sc 23 (60 st)

Round 38	Sc 60 (60 st)
Round 39	Sc 3, dec 3, sc 24, dec 3, sc 21 (54 st)
Round 40	Sc 54 (54 st)
Round 41	Sc 2, dec 3, sc 21, dec 3, sc 19 (48 st)
Round 42	Sc 1, dec 3, sc 18, dec 3, sc 17 (42 st)
Round 43	Sc 35 (35 st, 42 st total in round) *This round stops 7 st short of a full round to adjust the alignment, shift stitch marker accordingly*
Round 44	Sc 7, dec 3, sc 15, dec 3, sc 8 (36 st)
Round 45	Sc 6, dec 3, sc 12, dec 3, sc 6 (30 st)
Round 46	Sc 5, dec 3, sc 9, dec 3, sc 4 (24 st)
Round 47	Sc 24 (24 st)
Round 48	Sc 4, dec 3, sc 6, dec 3, sc 2 (18 st)
Round 49	[Sc 3, dec 3] 2x (12 st)
Round 50	Sc 12 (12 st)
Round 51	[Sc 2, dec] 3x (9 st)
Round 52	Sc 9 (9 st)
Round 53	[Sc 1, dec] 3x (6 st)
Round 54	Sc 6 (6 st)
Round 55	[Sc 1, dec] 2x (4 st)
Finishing Off	Cut and tie off, leaving VERY long tail for needle sculpting, sew remaining hole closed.

END RESULT

Needle Sculpting Spine Ridge & Flattening Shell cont.

After making the ridge, use the rest of your sewing tail to needle sculpt along the ridge, passing through the top and bottom layers of the shell and pulling the yarn snug. This should flatten the shell and make it easier to sew it to the body later on.

END RESULT

Needle Sculpting Spine Ridge & Flattening Shell

On one side of the shell, pinch the center of the shell from pointy tip to pointy tip, such that the amount of material that is being pinched is about 4 st wide. You don't want the ridge to be too tall.

Then, take your yarn tail and weave your needle back and forth at the base of where you've just pinched to needle sculpt this ridge into place; go from tip to tip. Refer to the photos to get a better visual idea of how this should look.

Helpful Hint: You can use clothespins or binder clips to keep the ridge in place as you sew!

BODY

Use **body color** yarn. You will be using the invisible join technique, which is described in the Terminology section of this book. Stuff the piece as you go.

Round 1	Ch 6, starting in 2nd ch from hook: sc 4, inc, continue along the bottom of the chains starting in the bottom of the inc stitch: sc 4, inc (12 st)
Round 2	Inc, sc 3, inc 3, sc 3, inc 2 (18 st)
Round 3	Sc 1, inc, sc 3, [sc 1, inc] 3x, sc 3, [sc 1, inc] 2x, invisible join, ch 1 (24 st)
Round 4	Bpsc 24, invisible join, ch 1 (24 st)
Technique Note	From this point on, work in **Front Loops Only** except for the bpsc stitches. This will prevent the seam of your join from twisting around.
Round 5-7	Sc 24, invisible join, ch 1 (24 st per round) (3 rounds)
Round 8	Bpsc 24, invisible join, ch 1 (24 st)
Round 9-11	Sc 24, invisible join, ch 1 (24 st per round) (3 rounds)
Round 12	Bpsc 24, invisible join, ch 1 (24 st)
Round 13-15	Sc 24, invisible join, ch 1 (24 st per round) (3 rounds)
Round 16	Bpsc 24, invisible join, ch 1 (24 st)
Round 17-19	Sc 24, invisible join, ch 1 (24 st per round) (3 rounds)
Round 20	Bpsc 24, invisible join, ch 1 (24 st)
Round 21-23	Sc 24, invisible join, ch 1 (24 st per round) (3 rounds)
Round 24	Bpsc 24, invisible join, ch 1 (24 st)
Round 25-27	Sc 24, invisible join, ch 1 (24 st per round) (3 rounds)
Round 28	Bpsc 24, invisible join, ch 1 (24 st)
Round 29-31	Sc 24, invisible join, ch 1 (24 st per round) (3 rounds)
Round 32	Bpsc 24, invisible join, ch 1 (24 st)
Technique Note	Cease working in **Front Loops Only** and begin working in spiral rounds again after completing Round 32.
Round 33	Sc 1, dec, sc 3, [sc 1, dec] 3x, sc 3, [sc 1, dec] 2x (18 st)
Round 34	Dec, sc 3, dec 3, sc 3, dec 2 (12 st)
Finishing Off	Slst to next st, cut and tie off a very long sewing tail, flatten the remaining hole and sew it closed in a line using whip stitch sewing technique in the front loops only for the cleanest seam. Keep the sewing tail on for the next step. The Round 1 side of the body will be the front.

END RESULT

SEWING BODY TO SHELL

Alignment	Place the body on the underside of the shell and face the front of the body with the front of the shell (Round 55 end). To use a geometry term, the major axis of the oval should be parallel with the major axis of the shell. The front of the body should be flush with the base of the pointed tips on both sides of the shell. Weave the yarn tail from the body to the side of the body so that it is in the proper position to begin sewing.
Sewing	Use seamless sewing technique all the way around the body wherever the two pieces meet. Make sure that Rounds 1-3 of the front of the body are completely free; you will need this to not be flattened down by sewing so that the eye stalks will fit.

EYE STALKS (MAKE 2)

Start with **eye color** yarn. You will switch to **main color** yarn when prompted. Stuff when finished.

Round 1	Ch 2, sc 6 in 2nd ch from hook (6 st)
Color Change	Switch to **main color** yarn.
Round 2	[Sc 1, inc] 3x (9 st)
Round 3	BLO: Slst, sc 8 (9 st) *Starting the first round of a new color with a slst makes the color transition smoother*
Round 4-8	BLO: Sc 9 (9 st per round) (5 rounds)
Round 9	BLO: [Sc 2, inc] 3x (12 st)
Finishing Off	Slst to next st, cut and tie off, leaving long tail for sewing, stuff the eye stalk.

END RESULT

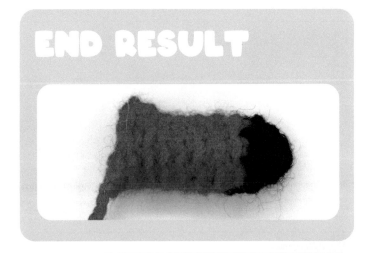

SEWING EYES TO BODY

Alignment	Place the open end of the eye stalk onto the front of the body and angle them so that they point outwards at an angle. See the reference photo for a better idea.
Sewing	Use seamless sewing technique.

LEG PIECES (MAKE 2)

Use **main color** yarn. You will be making 6 separate legs for each side of the body and then crocheting them together in numerical order into single pieces that will be easier to sew on. Don't stuff any of the legs.

Leg 1	
Round 1	Ch 2, sc 4 in 2nd ch from hook (4 st)
Round 2	Sc 4 (4 st)
Round 3	Inc, sc 3 (5 st)
Round 4-5	Sc 5 (5 st per round) (2 rounds)
Round 6	Sc 4, inc (6 st)
Round 7-8	Sc 6 (6 st per round) (2 rounds)
Finishing Off	Cut and tie off, weave in end.

END RESULT

Leg 2	
Round 1	Ch 2, sc 4 in 2nd ch from hook (4 st)
Round 2	Sc 4 (4 st)
Round 3	Inc, sc 3 (5 st)
Round 4-5	Sc 5 (5 st per round) (2 rounds)
Round 6	Sc 4, inc (6 st)

Round 7-11	Sc 6 (6 st per round) (5 rounds)
Finishing Off	Cut and tie off, weave in end.

END RESULT

Leg 4-5	Make 2
Round 1	Ch 2, sc 4 in 2nd ch from hook (4 st)
Round 2	Sc 4 (4 st)
Round 3	Inc, sc 3 (5 st)
Round 4-5	Sc 5 (5 st per round) (2 rounds)
Round 6	Sc 4, inc (6 st)
Round 7-16	Sc 6 (6 st per round) (10 rounds)
Finishing Off	Cut and tie off, weave in end.

END RESULT

Leg 6	
Round 1	Ch 2, sc 4 in 2nd ch from hook (4 st)
Round 2	Sc 4 (4 st)
Round 3	Inc, sc 3 (5 st)
Round 4-5	Sc 5 (5 st per round) (2 rounds)
Round 6	Sc 4, inc (6 st)
Round 7-18	Sc 6 (6 st per round) (12 rounds)
Round 19 (Joining Round)	Sc 3, ch 2, grab Leg 5 and continue in the first available stitch: sc 3, ch 2, Grab Leg 4 and continue in the first available stitch: sc 3, ch 2, Grab Leg 3 and continue in the first available stitch: sc 3, ch 2, Grab Leg 2 and continue in the first available stitch: sc 3, ch 2, Grab Leg 1 and continue in the first available stitch: sc 6, [Work in the back of the chains between the legs: sc 2, continue in next available stitch of the next leg: sc 3] 5x (56 st)
Finishing Off	Cut and tie off, weave in end.

END RESULT

ATTACHING LEGS TO BODY

Alignment	Place the opening of the leg piece against the side of the body. One leg should fit in the middle of each space between the bpsc rounds on the body. The one closest to the head will not have a leg. Place the shortest leg towards the front of the body, and make sure the leg piece is flush against the surface of the shell.
Sewing	Use seamless sewing technique.

TAIL PIECES (MAKE 2)

Use **tail color** yarn. Do not stuff these pieces.

Round 1	Ch 2, sc 4 in 2nd ch from hook (4 st)
Round 2-3	Sc 4 (4 st per round) (2 rounds)
Round 4	Inc, sc 3 (5 st)
Round 5-6	Sc 5 (5 st per round) (2 rounds)
Round 7	Inc, sc 4 (6 st)
Round 8-9	Sc 6 (6 st per round) (2 rounds)
Round 10	[Sc 2, inc] 2x (8 st)
Round 11-13	Sc 8 (8 st per round) (3 rounds)
*Row 14-15	Sc 4, ch 1 and turn (4 st per row) (2 rows)
Row 16	Sc 1, dec, sc 1, ch 1 and turn (3 st)
Row 17	Sc 3, ch 1 and turn (3 st)
Row 18	2/3 dec, ch 1 and turn (2 st)
Row 19	Sc 2, ch 1 and turn (2 st)
*Round 20	Dec, continue down the side of your work (working 1 sc into the side of each row): sc 6, drop down to unworked stitches of Round 13: sc 4, continue up the side of your work: sc 5, ch 2, slst in 2nd ch from hook, slst to the first stitch of this round (16 st, but stitch count is not too important. As long as you have a nice smooth edge, you're fine!)
Finishing Off	Cut and tie off, leaving long tail for sewing

END RESULT

ATTACHING TAIL PIECES TO SHELL

Alignment	Place the open end of the tail piece against the bottom surface of the shell so that the point of the tail piece is flush against the outer side of the Piece 1 & 3 parts of the shell. Refer to the photos for a better idea.
Sewing	Use <u>seamless sewing technique</u>.

FINAL PRODUCT

Your Duplapex is officially complete! Check out the gallery to the right to make sure your piece came out as intended.

GALLERY

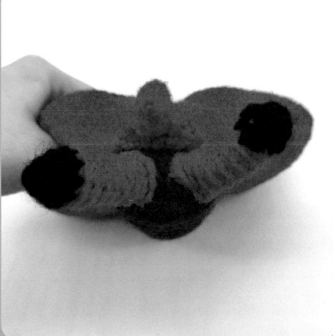

WAPTIA
(WOP-shuh)

MATERIALS

2.5 mm Crochet Hook (or hook size of your choice)
Yarn (All Worsted Weight):

Main Color	1/2 of a 364 yd skein
Fin Color	Less than 1/4 of a 364 yd skein
Eye Color	Only a few yards

Stuffing
Darning Needle
Stitch Marker
Sewing Pins

WHAT WAS WAPTIA?

Waptia was a shrimp-like arthropod that measured around 3 inches (6.6 cm) in length, but it was large enough to be a predator during this time! It likely ate soft-bodied prey.

Like most Cambrian fossils, Waptia was discovered in the Burgess Shale in British Columbia, Canada in the early 1900s. Waptia specifically was named after the nearby Wapta Mountain, with Wapta meaning "river" in the Stoney language spoken by a Dakotan group of First Nation's people from that part of Canada.

Waptia is one of the oldest known species of animal that shows direct evidence of brood care, which means that Waptia parents looked after Waptia babies until they were capable of surviving on their own!

The back plate on Waptia was not rigid and hard, but likely flexible. It also possessed several pairs of flaps behinds its legs. Some scientists believe that these enhanced Waptia's swimming abilities, while others believe they may have acted like gills. (There were quite a few unusual respiratory structures on animals during this time!)

This species is one of the most commonly found fossils in the Burgess Shale, making up around 2.5% of all specimens found, which is a lot when you consider just how many different life forms existed during the Cambrian! Waptia fossils are oftentimes found in pieces rather than whole.

No one knows for sure what led to the ultimate demise of Waptia, but it may have been one of the usual suspects: predation, environmental changes, or being out-competed for food.

Finished Size:
Approx. 17 in
(43 cm) long
from tail to antenna,
Results may vary
depending on
individual tension.

DIFFICULTY:

INTERMEDIATE

HEAD, BODY, & TAIL

Start with **main color** yarn. You will switch to **fin color** yarn towards the very end to make the two tail pieces. You will work the piece from head to tail. Stuff the whole piece as you go.

Round 1	Ch 2, sc 6 in 2nd ch from hook (6 st)
Round 2	Inc 6 (12 st)
Round 3	[Sc 1, inc] 6x (18 st)
Round 4	[Sc 2, inc] 6x (24 st)
Round 5	[Sc 3, inc] 6x (30 st)
Round 6-20	Sc 30 (30 st per round) (15 rounds)
Technique Note	From this point on for the rest of the Head/Body/Tail piece, you will work all regular sc stitches in the **Front Loops Only** (i.e. no bpsc or ddsc). This will prevent your rounds from slanting over time, which will help keep your curve work straight. DO NOT SKIP THIS STEP, your work will become twisted and warped if you don't do it!
Round 21	Slst 10, sc 20 (30 st)
Round 22	Ddsc 10, sc 20 (30 st)
Round 23	Sc 30 (30 st)
Round 24	Slst 10, sc 20 (30 st)
Round 25	Ddsc 10, sc 20 (30 st)
Round 26	Sc 30 (30 st)
Round 27	Slst 10, sc 20 (30 st)
Round 28	Ddsc 10, sc 20 (30 st)
Round 29-33	Sc 30 (30 st per round) (5 rounds) *After last round, invisible join to first st of the round and ch 1*

Round 34	*Always start a joined round in the same stitch that you joined to* Bpsc 30 (30 st) *Continue in spiral rounds in next round*
Round 35-40	Sc 30 (30 st per round) (6 rounds) *Invisible join after last round, ch 1*
Round 41	Bpsc 30 (30 st) *Continue in spiral rounds in next round*
Round 42	Sc 30 (30 st)
Round 43	Sc 15, slst 10, sc 5 (30 st)
Round 44	Sc 15, ddsc 10, sc 5 (30 st)
Round 45	Sc 30 (30 st)
Round 46	Sc 15, slst 10, sc 5 (30 st)
Round 47	Sc 15, ddsc 10, sc 5, invisible join, ch 1 (30 st)
Round 48	Bpsc 30 (30 st) *Continue in spiral rounds in next round*
Round 49	Sc 30 (30 st)
Round 50	Sc 15, slst 10, sc 5 (30 st)
Round 51	Sc 15, ddsc 10, sc 5 (30 st)
Round 52	Sc 30 (30 st)
Round 53	Sc 15, slst 10, sc 5 (30 st)
Round 54	Sc 15, ddsc 10, sc 5, invisible join, ch 1 (30 st)
Round 55	Bpsc 30 (30 st) *Continue in spiral rounds in next round*
Round 56-60	Sc 30 (30 st per round) (5 rounds)
Round 61	[Sc 3, dec] 6x, invisible join, ch 1 (24 st)
Round 62	Bpsc 24 (24 st) *Continue in spiral rounds in next round*
Round 63-67	Sc 24 (24 st per round) (5 rounds)
Round 68	[Sc 2, dec] 6x, invisible join, ch 1 (18 st)

Round 69	Bpsc 18 (18 st) *Continue in spiral rounds in next round*
Color Change	Switch to **fin color** yarn.
Round 70	Sc 5, skip 9 stitches, sc 4 (9 st) *You will be closing off the piece into a round of 9 st. You will continue working in FLO*
Round 71	Inc, sc 8 (10 st)
Round 72	Inc, sc 9 (11 st)
Round 73	Inc, sc 10 (12 st)
Round 74	Sc 1, inc, sc 10 (13 st)
Round 75	Sc 2, inc, sc 10 (14 st)
Round 76	Sc 3, inc, sc 10 (15 st)
Round 77	Sc 3, inc, sc 11 (16 st)
Round 78	Sc 4, inc, sc 11 (17 st)
Round 79	Sc 5, inc, sc 11 (18 st)
Round 80	Sc 4, dec, sc 7, dec, sc 3 (16 st)
Round 81	Sc 3, dec, sc 6, dec, sc 3 (14 st)
Round 82	Sc 2, dec, sc 5, dec, sc 3 (12 st)
Round 83	Dec 6 (6 st)
Round 84	[Sc 1, dec] 2x (4 st)
Finishing Off	Slst to next st, cut and tie off, sew remaining hole closed, weave in end.

END RESULT

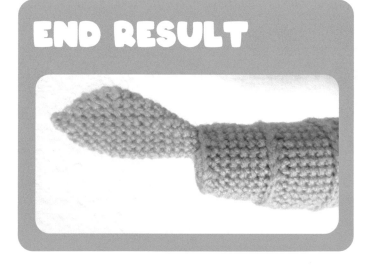

Reattaching for Second Fin	With your first tail piece to the right and the open hole to the left, reattach your **fin color** yarn to the very first available stitch to the left of the first tail piece (if you're left-handed, mirror these instructions). You will make your first stitch in this stitch. The rounds will continue at Round 85 instead of starting over. Continue working in FLO.
Round 85	Sc 9 (9 st)
Round 86	Starting in the first stitch of Round 85: sc 4, inc, sc 4 (10 st)
Round 87	Sc 5, inc, sc 4 (11 st)
Round 88	Sc 5, inc, sc 5 (12 st)
Round 89	Sc 5, inc, sc 6 (13 st)
Round 90	Sc 6, inc, sc 6 (14 st)
Round 91	Sc 6, inc, sc 7 (15 st)
Round 92	Sc 7, inc, sc 7 (16 st)
Round 93	Sc 8, inc, sc 7 (17 st)
Round 94	Sc 8, inc, sc 12 (22 st total, 18 st in round) *This round goes 4 st past a full round to shift alignment, move stitch marker accordingly*
Round 95	Sc 4, dec, sc 7, dec, sc 3 (16 st)
Round 96	Sc 3, dec, sc 6, dec, sc 3 (14 st)
Round 97	Sc 2, dec, sc 5, dec, sc 3 (12 st)
Round 98	Dec 6 (6 st)
Round 99	[Sc 1, dec] 2x (4 st)
Finishing Off	Slst to next st, cut and tie off, sew remaining hole closed, weave in end.

END RESULT

FINS (MAKE 8)

Use **fin color** yarn.

Row 1	Ch 9, starting in 2nd ch from hook: sc 7, inc, continue in the bottom of the chains starting in the chain that you worked the inc into: sc 8, ch 1 and turn (17 st)
Row 2	Sc 8, trp inc, sc 8, ch 1 and turn (19 st)
*Round 3	Sc 9, trp inc, sc 9, ch 1, continue along the flat side of your work (making 1 sc in the side of each row): sc 5, slst to first st of this round (26 st)
Finishing Off	Cut and tie off, weave in ends

END RESULT

LEFT-SIDE FIN PIECE

You will use **main color** yarn to crochet four fins together as specified below. Your result may be flipped if you are left-handed!

Alignment	Your four fins are going to overlap as shown below in the photo. The **leftmost** fin will be on top.
Crocheting Them Together	Attach your **main color** yarn to the rightmost of the 5 stitches along the flat edge of one of the fins (leftmost if you're left-handed). You will make your first stitch in this stitch. Sc in the first two stitches of the fin. Then, place the next fin (Fin 2) on top of the first fin (Fin 1) so that the last 3 stitches of Fin 1 overlap with the first 3 stitches of Fin 2. You will sc through the stitches of BOTH fins for a total of 2 sc.

	Then, add Fin 3 to the top of Fin 2 in the same over-lapping fashion (first 3 of new fin and last 3 stitches of the fin before it over-lapping). You will work 1 sc through the next available stitch of ALL THREE FINS (This will be the 5th stitch of Fin 1, 3rd stitch of Fin 2, and 1st stitch of Fin 3)
Crocheting Them Together cont.	Next, sc 1 through the next available stitches of both Fin 2 and Fin 3.
	Next, add Fin 4 to the top of Fin 3 in the same over-lapping fashion and sc 1 through the next available stitch of ALL THREE FINS (This will be the 5th stitch of Fin 2, 3rd stitch of Fin 3, and 1st stitch of Fin 4). Then, sc through the avail-able stitches of Fins 3 and 4 twice for a total of 2 sc 1, which will bring you to the end of Fin 3.
	Sc in the last two stitches of Fin 4 normally. (11 st)

END RESULT

RIGHT-SIDE FIN PIECE

You will use **main color** yarn to crochet four fins together as specified below. Your result may be flipped if you are left-handed!

Alignment	Your four fins are going to overlap as shown below in the photo. The **rightmost** fin will be on top.
Crocheting Them Together	Attach your **main color** yarn to the rightmost of the 5 stitches along the flat edge of one of the fins (leftmost if you're left-handed). You will make your first stitch in this stitch.
	Sc in each of the first two stitches of the fin. Then, place the next fin (Fin 2) UNDER the first fin (Fin 1) so that the last 3 stitches of Fin 1 overlap with the first 3 stitches of Fin 2. You will sc through the stitches of BOTH fins for a total of 2 sc.
	Then, add Fin 3 to the bottom of Fin 2 in the same overlapping fashion (first 3 of new fin and last 3 stitches of the fin before it overlapping). You will work 1 sc through the next available stitch of ALL THREE FINS (This will be the 5th stitch of Fin 1, 3rd stitch of Fin 2, and 1st stitch of Fin 3)
	Next, sc 1 through the next available stitches of both Fin 2 and 3.

Crocheting Them Together cont.	Next, add Fin 4 to the BOTTOM of Fin 3 in the same overlapping fashion and sc 1 through the next available stitch of ALL THREE FINS (This will be the 5th stitch of Fin 2, 3rd stitch of Fin 3, and 1st stitch of Fin 4). Then, sc through the next available stitches of Fin 3 and 4 twice for a total of 2 sc, which will bring you to the end of Fin 3. Sc in the last two stitches of Fin 4 normally (11 st)
Finishing Off	Cut and tie off, leaving long tail for sewing

END RESULT

LEG PIECES (MAKE 2)

Use **main color** yarn.

How to Work Leg Pieces	There will be 4 legs on each side of the body, and to make sewing much less tedious, we will be crocheting all of the legs on one side together into a single round. We will later sew on each four-legged piece as one. You will make Legs 1-3 and cut your yarn and tie them off. The fourth leg, however, you will keep your yarn active. From here, you will work into the other three legs as specified later in the pattern.
Leg 1	
Round 1	Ch 2, sc 6 in 2nd ch from hook (6 st)
Round 2-13	Sc 6 (6 st per round) (12 rounds)
Finishing Off	Cut and tie off, weave in end.

END RESULT

Leg 2	
Round 1	Ch 2, sc 6 in 2nd ch from hook (6 st)
Round 2-11	Sc 6 (6 st per round) (10 rounds)
Finishing Off	Cut and tie off, weave in end.

END RESULT

Leg 3	
Round 1	Ch 2, sc 6 in 2nd ch from hook (6 st)
Round 2-9	Sc 6 (6 st per round) (8 rounds)
Finishing Off	Cut and tie off, weave in end.

END RESULT

Leg 4	
Round 1	Ch 2, sc 6 in 2nd ch from hook (6 st)
Round 2-7	Sc 6 (6 st per round) (6 rounds)

Leg Joining Round	Your active loop should be in Leg 4, but your first stitch will be in Leg 3. Starting in the first available stitch of Leg 3: sc 3, starting in the first available stitch of Leg 2: sc 3, starting in the first available slitch of Leg 1: sc 6, return to next available stitch of Leg 2: sc 3, return to next available stitch of Leg 3: sc 3, return to next available stitch of Leg 4: sc 6 (24 st)
Finishing Off	Slst to next st, cut and tie off, leaving long tail for sewing

END RESULT

EYES (MAKE 2)

Start with **eye color** yarn. You will switch to **body color** yarn when prompted.

Round 1	Ch 2, sc 6 in 2nd ch from hook (6 st)
Round 2-3	Sc 6 (6 st per round) (2 rounds)
Color Change	Switch to body color yarn.

Round 4	BLO: slst, dec, sc 1, dec (4 st) *Starting the first round of a new color with a slst makes the color transition smoother. You will work into it as normal in the next round*
Round 5	Sc 4 (4 st)
Round 6	[Sc 1, inc] 2x (6 st)
Round 7	Sc 6 (6 st)
Finishing Off	Slst to next st, cut and tie off, leaving long tail for sewing

END RESULT

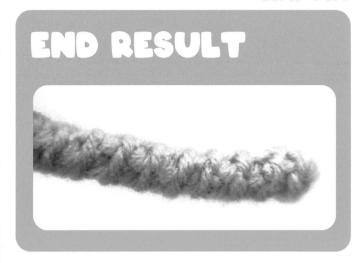

END RESULT

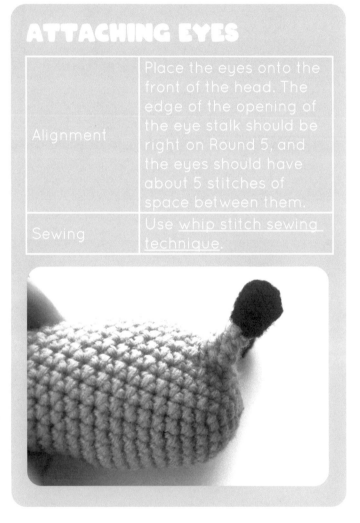

ANTENNAE (MAKE 2)

Use **body color** yarn.

Round 1	Ch 2, sc 4 in 2nd ch from hook (4 st)
Round 2-11	BLO: sc 4 (4 st per round) (10 rounds) *Working in the back loops only will give a ridged texture*
Finishing Off	Slst to next st, cut and tie off, leaving long tail for sewing

ATTACHING EYES

Alignment	Place the eyes onto the front of the head. The edge of the opening of the eye stalk should be right on Round 5, and the eyes should have about 5 stitches of space between them.
Sewing	Use whip stitch sewing technique.

ATTACHING ANTENNAE

Alignment	Place the antennae between the eyes and about two rounds down. They should be right up against the Round 1 of the body.
Sewing	Use <u>whip stitch sewing technique</u>.

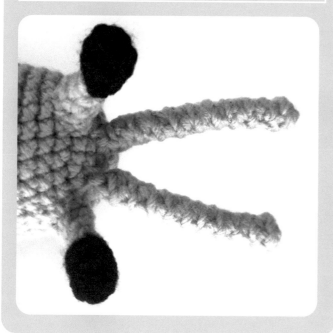

ATTACHING LEGS

Alignment	Place the legs against the body with the shortest leg closest to the front of the head. The frontmost leg, if vertically aligned with the eye stalks, would be right next to each other, but you will drop them down about 4-5 stitches lower than the eye stalks. Along the bottom side, there should be about 7 stitches of space between the frontmost legs and about 10 stitches of space between the backmost legs.
Sewing	Use <u>whip stitch sewing technique</u>.

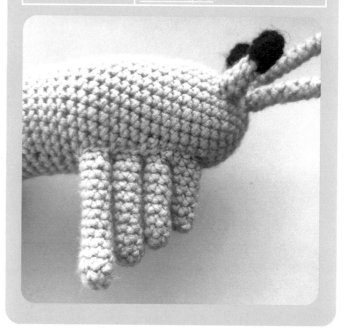

ATTACHING FINS

Alignment	The front edge of the fin piece should be right up against the backmost of the legs. The piece will have a natural curve to it; allow the piece to curve slightly upward so that the fins will spread nicely. The back end of the fin piece should be right up against the first back post ridge of the body.
Sewing	Use whip stitch sewing technique.

BACK PLATE

Use **main color** yarn.

Row 1	Ch 7, starting in 2nd ch from hook: sc 5, inc, ch 1 and turn (7 st)
Row 2	Inc, sc 6, ch 1 and turn (8 st)
Row 3	Sc 7, inc, ch 1 and turn (9 st)
Row 4	Inc, sc 8, ch 1 and turn (10 st)
Row 5	Sc 9, inc, ch 1 and turn (11 st)
Row 6	Inc, sc 10, ch 1 and turn (12 st)
Row 7	Sc 11, inc, ch 1 and turn (13 st)
Row 8	Inc, sc 12, ch 1 and turn (14 st)
Row 9	Sc 13, inc, ch 1 and turn (15 st)
Row 10	Inc, sc 14, ch 1 and turn (16 st)

Row 11	Dec, sc 14, ch 1 and turn (15 st)
Row 12	Sc 13, dec, ch 1 and turn (14 st)
Row 13	Dec, sc 12, ch 1 and turn (13 st)
Row 14	Sc 11, dec, ch 1 and turn (12 st)
Row 15	Dec, sc 10, ch 1 and turn (11 st)
Row 16	Sc 9, dec, ch 1 and turn (10 st)
Row 17	Dec, sc 8, ch 1 and turn (9 st)
Row 18	Sc 8, inc, ch 1 and turn (10 st)
Row 19	Inc, sc 9, ch 1 and turn (11 st)
Row 20	Sc 10, inc, ch 1 and turn (12 st)
Row 21	Inc, sc 11, ch 1 and turn (13 st)
Row 22	Sc 12, inc, ch 1 and turn (14 st)
Row 23	Inc, sc 13, ch 1 and turn (15 st)
Row 24	Sc 14, inc, ch 1 and turn (16 st)
Row 25	Sc 14, dec, ch 1 and turn (15 st)
Row 26	Dec, sc 13, ch 1 and turn (14 st)
Row 27	Sc 12, dec, ch 1 and turn (13 st)
Row 28	Dec, sc 11, ch 1 and turn (12 st)
Row 29	Sc 10, dec, ch 1 and turn (11 st)
Row 30	Dec, sc 9, ch 1 and turn (10 st)
Row 31	Sc 8, dec, ch 1 and turn (9 st)
Row 32	Dec, sc 7, ch 1 and turn (8 st)

Row 33	Sc 6, dec, ch 1 and turn (7 st)
Row 34	Dec, sc 5, ch 1 and turn (6 st)
*Round 35	Sc 6, continue down the side of your work (working 1 sc in the side of each row): sc 34, continue in the bottom of the stitches from Row 1: inc, sc 5, continue down the side of your work: sc 35, slst to first stitch of this round (82 st) *If your stitch count is not exactly right, don't worry. This is just to give the piece a smooth edge, as long as it lays flat you're fine!*
Finishing Off	Cut and tie off, leaving long tail for sewing, weave in starting end tail

END RESULT

ATTACHING BACK PLATE TO BODY

Alignment	Place the piece over the body so that the flat edge is about 2-3 rounds back from the eyes, and the side that concaves inward is facing towards the back.
Sewing	Use <u>invisible sewing technique</u> around the perimeter of the back plate, going through whatever part of the body that the back plate touches (i.e. parts of the fins, back, and legs)

FINAL PRODUCT

Your Waptia is officially complete! Check out the gallery to the right to make sure your piece came out as intended.

ANOMALOCARIS

(Uh-NOM-uh-low-CAR-iss)

MATERIALS

2.5 mm Crochet Hook (or hook size of your choice)
Yarn (All Worsted Weight):

Main Color	About 1/2 of a 364 yd skein
Fin Color	Less than 1/2 of a 364 yd skein
Tail Color	Less than 1/4 of a 364 yd skein
Eye Color	Only a few yards

Stuffing
Stem Wire
Darning Needle
Stitch Marker
Sewing Pins

WHAT WAS ANOMALOCARIS?

Anomalocaris, whose name means "weird shrimp", was the bad boy of the Cambrian Period. It was Earth's first known "apex predator", reaching lengths of 1.25 ft (38 cm) long, which was quite large during this era. (Size estimates are a hot topic.) Your Anomalocaris should be about life sized!

It belonged to the order *Radiodonta* (meaning "round tooth"), which dominated the top of the Cambrian food chain.

This giant shrimp predator used its front appendages to grasp its prey and draw it into its mouth. It most likely hunted soft-bodied prey, but some scientists believe it may have been able to pierce through the shells of trilobites. It traveled through the water by undulating the overlapping flaps on the sides of its body, making it a very effective swimmer. One of its most notable features is its set of compound eyes, a trait that was very new during this time. Compound eyes are what you see when you look at a house fly's eye: it contains thousands of tiny photoreceptor cells that gave it exceptional vision compared to most other life during the Cambrian. Creatures like the Five-Eyed Opabinia could only detect very simple visual elements, such as moving shadows. Many animals at this time had no eyes at all, so this put Anomalocaris in a highly advantageous position.

Anomalocaris existed for about 20 million years, and the fossil records show that as the years went on, Anomalocaris seemed to have doubled in size. Some scientists believe that these larger specimens may have been a different species of Anomalocaris, but this idea is hotly contested. It likely lived in shallow tropical waters in what is now China and Australia.

Finished Size:
Approx. 15 in
(38 cm) long
from head to tail,
Results may vary
depending on
individual tension.

DIFFICULTY:

INTERMEDIATE

HEAD & BODY

Use **main color** yarn. Stuff the piece as you go.

OPTIONAL STEM WIRE: Whenever you feel the time is right, you can place a length of stem wire (12"/30 cm) into the body to make it poseable. I inserted mine around Round 42. It should be against the inner surface of the body and not in the dead center. If there is too much stuffing around it, it will not bend as well. Make sure you have more than enough stem wire hanging out so that it will be enough to run the entire length of the piece. It is better to have more than you need and trim it towards the end.

Round 1	Ch 6, starting in 2nd ch from hook: sc 4, inc, continue along the bottom starting in the bottom of the stitch you just made your inc into: sc 4, inc (12 st)
Round 2	Inc, sc 3, inc 3, sc 3, inc 2 (18 st)
Round 3	Sc 1, inc, sc 3, [sc 1, inc] 3x, sc 3, [sc 1, inc] 2x (24 st)
Round 4-13	Sc 24 (24 st per round) (10 rounds) *After last round, invisible join, ch 1
Round 14	Bpsc 24 (24 st) *Continue in spiral rounds again*
Round 15	Sc 1, inc, sc 11, inc, sc 10 (26 st)
Round 16	Sc 26 (26 st)
Round 17	Sc 1, inc, sc 12, inc, sc 11 (28 st)
Round 18	Sc 28 (28 st)
Round 19	Sc 3, inc, sc 13, inc, sc 10 (30 st)
Round 20	Sc 30, invisible join to first st, ch 1 (30 st)
Round 21	Start in the first stitch that you joined to: Bpsc 30 (30 st) *Continue in spiral rounds again*
Round 22	Sc 3, inc, sc 14, inc, sc 11 (32 st)
Round 23	Sc 32 (32 st)
Round 24	Sc 4, inc, sc 15, inc, sc 11 (34 st)
Round 25	Sc 34 (34 st)
Round 26	Sc 5, inc, sc 16, inc, sc 11 (36 st)
Round 27	Sc 36, invisible join to first st, ch 1 (36 st)
Round 28	Start in the first stitch that you joined to: Bpsc 36 (36 st) *Continue in spiral rounds again*
Round 29-34	Sc 36 (36 st per round) (6 rounds) *After last round, invisible join, ch 1*
Round 35	Start in the first stitch that you joined to: Bpsc 36 (36 st) *Continue in spiral rounds again*
Round 36-41	Sc 36 (36 st per round) (6 rounds) *After last round, invisible join, ch 1*
Round 42	Start in the first stitch that you joined to: Bpsc 36 (36 st) *Continue in spiral rounds again*
Stem Wire (Optional)	Follow the guidance under the "Head & Body" heading for specifics.
Round 43	Sc 9, dec, sc 16, dec, sc 7 (34 st)
Round 44	Sc 34 (34 st)
Round 45	Sc 9, dec, sc 15, dec, sc 6 (32 st)
Round 46	Sc 32 (32 st)
Round 47	Sc 8, dec, sc 14, dec, sc 6, invisible join to first st, ch 1 (30 st)

Round 48	Start in the first stitch that you joined to: Bpsc 30 (30 st) *Continue in spiral rounds again*
Round 49	Sc 8, dec, sc 13, dec, sc 5 (28 st)
Round 50	Sc 28 (28 st)
Round 51	Sc 9, dec, sc 12, dec, sc 3 (26 st)
Round 52	Sc 26 (26 st)
Round 53	Sc 8, dec, sc 11, dec, sc 3 (24 st)
Round 54	Sc 24, invisible join to first st, ch 1 (24 st)
Round 55	Start in the first stitch that you joined to: Bpsc 24 (24 st) *Continue in spiral rounds again*
Round 56	Sc 8, dec, sc 10, dec, sc 2 (22 st)
Round 57	Sc 22 (22 st)
Round 58	Sc 8, dec, sc 9, dec, sc 1 (20 st)
Round 59	Sc 20 (20 st)
Round 60	[Sc 8, dec] 2x (18 st)
Round 61	Sc 18 (18 st)
Round 62	[Dec, sc 7] 2x (16 st)
Round 63	Sc 16 (16 st)
Round 64	[Dec, sc 6] 2x (14 st)
Round 65	Sc 14 (14 st)
Round 66	[Dec, sc 5] 2x (12 st)
Round 67	Sc 12 (12 st)
Round 68	[Sc 2, dec] 3x (9 st)
Round 69	Sc 9 (9 st)
Round 70	[Sc 1, Dec] 3x (6 st)
Round 71	Sc 6 (6 st)
Finishing Off	Slst to next st, cut and tie off, sew remaining hole closed, weave in end

END RESULT

MANDIBLES (MAKE 2)

Use **tail color** yarn. Do not stuff this piece.

Round 1	Ch 2, sc 4 in 2nd ch from hook (4 st)
Round 2	[Sc 1, inc] 2x (6 st)
Round 3	BLO: Sc 6 (6 st)
Round 4	Slst 2, sc 4 (6 st)
Round 5	Ddsc 2, BLO: sc 4 (6 st)
Round 6	[Sc 1, inc] 3x (9 st)
Round 7	BLO: Slst 3, sc 6 (9 st)
Round 8	Ddsc 3, sc 6 (9 st)
Round 9	BLO: Sc 9 (9 st)
Round 10	Slst 3, sc 6 (9 st)
Round 11	Ddsc 3, BLO: sc 6 (9 st)
Round 12	Sc 10 (10 st total, 9 st in round) *This round goes one stitch past a full round to adjust alignment, shift stitch marker accordingly*
Round 13	BLO: Slst 3, sc 6
Round 14	Ddsc 3, sc 6 (9 st)
Round 15	BLO: Sc 9 (9 st)
Round 16	Slst 3, sc 6 (9 st)
Round 17	Ddsc 3, BLO: sc 6 (9 st)

| Finishing Off | Slst to next st, cut and tie off, leaving long tail for sewing. OPTIONAL: Insert stem wire into the mandible and leave about half an inch sticking out. You will push this into the stitches of the head to make the joint more stable. I recommend tightly wrapping the exposed end with Scotch tape to make insertion easier. |

END RESULT

ATTACHING MANDIBLES TO HEAD

| Alignment | Insert the stem wire of the mandibles just below the edges of each side of Round 1 (The foci of the oval to use a mathematical term) |
| Sewing | Use seamless sewing technique. |

EYES (MAKE 2)

Start with __eye color__ yarn. You will switch to __main color__ yarn when prompted. Stuff the piece as you go.

Round 1	Ch 2, sc 6 in 2nd ch from hook (6 st)
Round 2	Inc 6 (12 st)
Color Change	Switch to __main color__ yarn
Round 3	BLO: Slst, sc 11 (12 st) *Starting the first round of a new color with a slst makes the color transition smoother, work into it like a normal sc stitch*

Round 4	[Sc 2, dec] 3x (9 st)
Round 5-6	Sc 9 (9 st per round) (2 rounds)
Round 7	[Sc 1, dec] 3x (6 st)
Round 8-9	Sc 6 (6 st per round) (2 rounds)
Round 10	[Sc 1, inc] 3x (9 st)
Finishing Off	Slst to next st, cut and tie off, leaving long tail for sewing

END RESULT

ATTACHING EYES TO HEAD

Alignment	Place the eyes towards the front of the head and aligned over the mandibles below.
Sewing	Use whip stitch sewing technique.

MOUTH PIECE

Use **main color** yarn.

Explanation	You are going to be working far too many stitches than would normally fit into the round to achieve a specific look. Once you hit 6 sc in the round, you will continue making sc stitches in the starting chain space that enclose the stitches made before it. As you go, you will have to make your stitches bigger and bigger to encase the stitches you have made inside this chain space. The result will be a thick doughnut shape.
Round 1	Ch 2, sc 24 in the 2nd ch from hook (24 st)
Finishing Off	Slst to next st, cut and tie off, leaving long tail for sewing, weave in the other end.

END RESULT

ATTACHING MOUTH PIECE TO HEAD

Alignment	Place the mouth piece on the bottom of the head about one round back from the edge where the mandibles join to the head. Make sure that the "right side" of the work is against the surface of the head and the "wrong side" is facing outward.
Sewing	Use whip stitch sewing technique.

SIDE FLAP PIECES (MAKE 2)

Use **fin color** yarn. You will switch to **main color** yarn when prompted. You will be making five flap pieces per side (total of ten) and crocheting them together into single pieces to make sewing more efficient. The flaps are numbered and will be crocheted together in numerical order. Do not stuff.

Flap 3	
Round 1	Ch 2, sc 6 in 2nd ch from hook (6 st)
Round 2	Sc 6 (6 st)
Round 3	[Sc 1, inc] 3x (9 st)
Round 4	[Sc 2, inc] 3x (12 st)
Round 5	Sc 12 (12 st)
Round 6	[Sc 1, inc] 6x (18 st)
Round 7-18	Sc 18 (18 st per round) (12 rounds)
Finishing Off	Cut and tie off, weave in end.

END RESULT

Flap 5	
Round 1	Ch 2, sc 6 in 2nd ch from hook (6 st)
Round 2	Sc 6 (6 st)
Round 3	[Sc 1, inc] 3x (9 st)
Round 4	[Sc 2, inc] 3x (12 st)
Round 5	Sc 12 (12 st)
Round 6	[Sc 1, inc] 6x (18 st)
Round 7-11	Sc 18 (18 st per round) (5 rounds)
Finishing Off	Cut and tie off, weave in end.

Flap 2 & 4	Make 2 of these
Round 1	Ch 2, sc 6 in 2nd ch from hook (6 st)
Round 2	Sc 6 (6 st)
Round 3	[Sc 1, inc] 3x (9 st)
Round 4	[Sc 2, inc] 3x (12 st)
Round 5	Sc 12 (12 st)
Round 6	[Sc 1, inc] 6x (18 st)
Round 7-14	Sc 18 (18 st per round) (8 rounds)
Finishing Off	Cut and tie off, weave in end.

END RESULT

END RESULT

Flap 1	Do not cut and tie off after Round 11, keep your hook active in the piece
Round 1	Ch 2, sc 6 in 2nd ch from hook (6 st)
Round 2	Sc 6 (6 st)
Round 3	[Sc 1, inc] 3x (9 st)
Round 4	[Sc 2, inc] 3x (12 st)
Round 5	Sc 12 (12 st)
Round 6	[Sc 1, inc] 6x (18 st)
Round 7-11	Sc 18 (18 st per round) (5 rounds)

Joining Round	Starting in Flap 1: sc 9, continue in the next available stitch of Flap 2: sc 9, continue in the next available stitch of Flap 3: sc 9, continue in the next available stitch of Flap 4: sc 9, continue in the next available stitch of Flap 5: sc 18, continue in the next available stitch of Flap 4: sc 9, continue in the next available stitch of Flap 3: sc 9, continue in the next available stitch of Flap 2: sc 9, continue in the next available stitch of Flap 1: sc 9 (90 st)
Finishing Off	Slst to next st, cut and tie off, leaving long tail for sewing

Sewing	Use seamless sewing technique. Do not stuff the flaps.

END RESULT

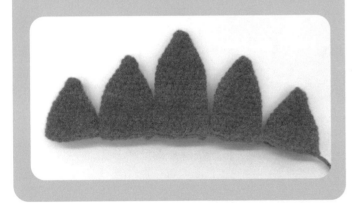

ATTACHING FLAP PIECES TO BODY

Alignment	Place the opening of the flap pieces on the sides of the body, centering it between the tip of the head and the tip of the tail.

TAIL PIECES (MAKE 2)

Use **tail color** yarn. You will be making two pieces for each side (total of four) and crocheting them together into one piece the same way you did with the flap pieces.

Piece 1	
Round 1	Ch 6, starting in 2nd ch from hook: sc 4, inc, continue along the bottom of your stitches starting in the bottom of the inc you just made: sc 4, inc (12 st)
Round 2	Sc 12 (12 st)
Round 3	Sc 13 (13 st total, 12 st in round) *This round goes 1 st past a full round to shift alignment, shift stitch marker accordingly*

Round 4	[Sc 4, dec] 2x (10 st)
Round 5-7	Sc 10 (10 st per round) (3 rounds)
Round 8	[Dec, sc 3] 2x (8 st)
Round 9-13	Sc 8 (8 st per round) (5 rounds) *After finishing the last round, ch 1 and turn*
*Row 14	Sc 6, ch 1 and turn (6 st)
Row 15	Sc 4, ch 1 and turn (4 st)
Row 16	Sc 2, ch 1 and turn (2 st)
*Round 17	Sc 2, [drop down to unworked stitches of row below: sc 2] 2x, go up to unworked stitches of row above: sc 2 (8 st)
Finishing Off	Cut and tie off, weave in end

END RESULT

Round 4	[Sc 4, dec] 2x (10 st)
Round 5-7	Sc 10 (10 st per round) (3 rounds)
Round 8	[Dec, sc 3] 2x (8 st)
Round 9-13	Sc 8 (8 st per round) (5 rounds) *After finishing the last round, ch 1 and turn*
*Row 14	Sc 6, ch 1 and turn (6 st)
Row 15	Sc 4, ch 1 and turn (4 st)
Row 16	Sc 2, ch 1 and turn (2 st)
*Round 17	Sc 2, [drop down to unworked stitches of row below: sc 2] 2x, go up to unworked stitches of row above: sc 2 (8 st)
Joining Round	Sc in the first 4 stitches of Piece 2, then working in the first available stitch of Piece 1 (making sure that they are both facing the same direction): sc 8 around, then return to Piece 2 and sc 1 in each of the last 4 stitches (16 st)
Finishing Off	Cut and tie off, weave in end

Piece 2	
Round 1	Ch 6, starting in 2nd ch from hook: sc 4, inc, continue along the bottom of your stitches starting in the bottom of the inc you just made: sc 4, inc (12 st)
Round 2	Sc 12 (12 st)
Round 3	Sc 13 (13 st total, 12 st in round) *This round goes 1 st past a full round to shift alignment, shift stitch marker accordingly*
Round 4	[Sc 4, dec] 2x (10 st)

END RESULT

ATTACHING TAIL PIECES TO BODY

Alignment	Place the opening of the tail pieces against the side of the tail in line with the flap pieces. Make sure the Round 1 side is pointing towards the back of the animal.
Sewing	Use whip stitch sewing technique.

FINAL PRODUCT

Your Anomalocaris is officially complete! Check out the gallery to the right to make sure your piece came out as intended.

GALLERY

SIDNEYIA
(SID-nee-uh)

MATERIALS

2.5 mm Crochet Hook (or hook size of your choice)
Yarn (All Worsted Weight):

Main Color	About one 364 yd skein
Body Color	Less than 1/2 of a 364 yd skein
Leg Color	Less than 1/4 of a 364 yd skein
Tail Color	Only a few yards

Stuffing
One Pair of 12 mm Safety Eyes
Darning Needle
Stitch Marker
Sewing Pins

WHAT WAS SIDNEYIA?

Sidneyia was a species of arthropod that was named after paleontologist Charles Walcott's son, Sidney. The species was actually discovered on day one of his expedition to the Burgess Shale and was the first fossil discovered at this iconic site.

As of now there are around 200 specimens that have been discovered worldwide. Walcott discovered Sidneyia in the Burgess Shale formation, but some have also been found in China; both locations are hot spots for Cambrian fossils.

For a Cambrian creature, it was a rather decent size, with the Sidneyia Inexpectans species reaching around 6 inches (15 mm) long, though the lesser known Sidneyia Malongensis was much smaller.

Sidneyia most likely scuttled around on the sea floor preying or scavenging on smaller arthropods. Scientists believe it may have been durophagous, which is an eating behavior in which an animal has extra jaw strength that can crush through bones, shells, and other hard substances. The Giant Panda is a modern day example of durophagy.

Sidneyia possessed a set of gills, but they are quite different than the gills we are used to today. It had a few sets of small limbs behinds its antennae that scientists believe may have helped it breathe.

Some fossils of Sidneyia have their stomach contents intact and include animals such as trilobites and clam-like bivalve creatures. Unfortunately, Sidneyia is one of the lesser known species from the Cambrian Explosion, so not too much is really known about them.

Finished Size:
Approx. 14 in
(35 cm) long
from head to tail,
Results may vary
depending on
individual tension.

DIFFICULTY:

ADVANCED INTERMEDIATE

HEAD

Use **main color** yarn. Do not stuff for now. This will be worked in an oval, there are many great guides online if you have never done it before! Stuff the piece lightly at the end.

Round 1	Ch 12, starting in 2nd ch from hook: sc 10, inc, continue along the bottom of your work starting in the bottom of the inc stitch: sc 10, inc (24 st)
Round 2	Inc, sc 9, inc 3, sc 9, inc 2 (30 st)
Round 3	Sc 1, inc, sc 9, [sc 1, inc] 3x, sc 9, [sc 1, inc] 2x (36 st)
Round 4	Sc 2, inc, sc 9, [sc 2, inc] 3x, sc 9, [sc 2, inc] 2x (42 st)
Round 5	Sc 3, inc, sc 9, [sc 3, inc] 3x, sc 9, [sc 3, inc] 2x (48 st)
Round 6-10	Sc 48 (48 st per round) (5 rounds)
*Row 11	Sc 28, ch 1 and turn (28 st)
Row 12	Sc 33, ch 1 and turn (33 st)
Row 13	Sc 31, ch 1 and turn (31 st)
Row 14	Sc 29 (29 st)
Finishing Off	Cut and tie off, weave in end

END RESULT

Reattaching Yarn	Go to the 15 unworked stitches from Round 10 and mark the 5th stitch from the right, shown marked by a stitch marker in the photo below. You will reattach your yarn to this stitch, and your first stitch of the new round will be made in this stitch.
Row 1	Sc 7, ch 1 and turn (7 st)
Row 2	Dec, sc 3, dec, ch 1 and turn (5 st)
Row 3	Dec, sc 1, dec, ch 1 and turn (3 st)
Row 4	Trp dec, ch 1 and turn (1 st)
*Round 5	Sc 1, continue down the side of your work putting 1 sc into the side of each row: sc 3, continue in unworked stitches from Round 10: sc 4, go up to unworked stitches of row above: sc 2, go up to unworked stitches of row above: sc 29, drop down to unworked stitches of row below: sc 2, drop down to unworked stitches of Round 10: sc 4, continue up the side of the triangle piece: sc 4 (49 st)
*Row 6	Start in the first stitch of Round 5: inc, sc 15, ch 1 and turn (17 st)
Row 7	Sc 8, turn without chaining (8 st)
Row 8	Skip first two stitches, sc 6, ch 1 and turn (6 st)
Row 9	Sc 8, turn without chaining (8 st) *For each of these "turn without chaining" rows, the last two stitches will have you dropping down to the next available stitch of Row 6*

Row 10-27	For every even row, repeat Row 8 (9 even rows) For every odd row, repeat Row 9 (9 odd rows) (18 total rows)
Row 28	Skip first two stitches, sc 6 (6 st)
Row 29	Flip the entire piece inside out. Then, line up the 6 stitches of Row 28 with the first 6 available unworked stitches of Round 10 of the head, shown in the photo below. Then sc through both the Row 28 stitch and the corresponding Round 10 stitch directly behind it (repeat this 6 times for a total of 6 stitches)
Finishing Off	Flip the piece back to right side out, cut and tie off, weave in ends. DO NOT SEW THE REMAINING HOLE CLOSED.

END RESULT

ATTACHING SAFETY EYES

Placement	Place one safety eye on the far edge of each side of the head between Rounds 8 and 9. Then, lightly stuff the head, just enough to keep its shape.

BACK PLATE

Use **main color** yarn. Do not stuff, this piece will stay flat. See "invisible join" in terminology page for tutorial.

Round 1	Ch 12, starting in 2nd ch from hook: sc 10, inc, continue along the bottom of your work starting in the bottom of the inc stitch: sc 10, inc (24 st)
Round 2	Inc, sc 9, inc 3, sc 9, inc 2 (30 st)
Round 3	Sc 1, inc, sc 9, [sc 1, inc] 3x, sc 9, [sc 1, inc] 2x (36 st)
Round 4	Sc 2, inc, sc 9, [sc 2, inc] 3x, sc 9, [sc 2, inc] 2x (42 st)
Round 5	Sc 3, inc, sc 9, [sc 3, inc] 3x, sc 9, [sc 3, inc] 2x (48 st)
Round 6	Sc 4, inc, sc 9, [sc 4, inc] 3x, sc 9, [sc 4, inc] 2x (54 st)
Round 7-10	Sc 54 (54 st per round) (4 rounds)
Round 11	Sc 54, invisible join to first stitch, ch 1 (54 st)
Round 12	Bpsc 54 (54 st) *Return to working in spiral rounds in next round*
Round 13	[Sc 2, inc] 2x, sc 9, [sc 2, inc] 6x, sc 9, [sc 2, inc] 4x (66 st)
Round 14-16	Sc 66 (66 st per round) (3 rounds)
Round 17	Sc 66, invisible join to first stitch of this round, ch 1 (66 st)
Round 18	Bpsc 66 (66 st) *Return to spiral rounds in next round*
Round 19	[Sc 3, inc] 2x, sc 9, [sc 3, inc] 6x, sc 9, [sc 3, inc] 4x (78 st)
Round 20-22	Sc 78 (78 st per round) (3 rounds)
Round 23	Sc 78, invisible join to first stitch of this round, ch 1 (78 st)
Round 24	Bpsc 78 (78 st) *Return to spiral rounds in next round*
Round 25-28	Sc 78 (78 st per round) (4 rounds)
Round 29	Sc 78, invisible join to first stitch, ch 1 (78 st)
Round 30	Bpsc 78 (78 st) *Return to spiral rounds in next round*
Round 31-34	Sc 78 (78 st per round) (4 rounds)
Round 35	Sc 78, invisible join to first stitch, ch 1 (78 st)
Round 36	Bpsc 78 (78 st) *Return to spiral rounds in next round*
Round 37	Sc 5, [sc 3, dec] 2x, sc 9, [sc 3, dec] 6x, sc 9, [sc 3, dec] 4x (71 st total, 66 st in the round) *This round goes 5 stitches past a full round to shift alignment, shift stitch marker accordingly*
Round 38-40	Sc 66 (66 st per round) (3 rounds)
Round 41	Sc 66, invisible join to first stitch, ch 1 (66 st)
Round 42	Bpsc 66 (66 st) *Return to spiral rounds in next round*
Round 43	Sc 2, [Sc 2, dec] 2x, sc 9, [sc 2, dec] 6x, sc 9, [sc 2, dec] 4x (56 st total, 54 st in the round) *This round will go two stitches, or one decrease, past a full round to shift the alignment of the beginning of the round*
Round 44-46	Sc 54 (54 st per round) (3 rounds)
Round 47	Sc 54, invisible join to first stitch, ch 1 (54 st)
Round 48	Bpsc 54 (54st) *Return to spiral rounds in next round*

Round 49	[Sc 1, dec] 2x, sc 9, [sc 1, dec] 6x, sc 9, [sc 1, dec] 4x (42 st)
Round 50-53	Sc 42 (42 st per round) (4 rounds)
Finishing Off	Slst to next st, cut and tie off, leaving a long tail for sewing. Flatten the piece, then use the yarn tail to sew the remaining hole shut with zigzag sewing technique.

END RESULT

TAIL

Start with **main color** yarn. You will switch to **tail color** towards the end to make the tail fan. Do not stuff this piece, it will lay flat.
When you make your slip knot, make sure you leave a long yarn tail. This will make sewing easier later on

Round 1	Ch 24, slst to the furthest chain from hook, ch 1, then start in the same ch you just slip stitched into: sc 24 around, invisible join to first st, ch 1 (24 st)

Round 2-5	Start in the same stitch that you just joined to: sc 24, invisible join to first st, ch 1 (24 st per round) (4 rounds)
Round 6	Bpsc 24, invisible join to first st, ch 1 (24 st)
Round 7	[Sc 2, dec] 6x, invisible join to first st, ch 1 (18 st)
Round 8-11	Sc 18, invisible join to first st, ch 1 (18 st per round) (4 rounds)
Round 12	Bpsc 18 (18 st) *Stop joining at the end of your rounds after this point*
Color Change	Switch to **tail color** yarn.
Round 13	Sc 1, trp inc, sc 8, trp inc, sc 7 (22 st)
Technique Note	From this point onward, work only in the Front Loops Only. This will keep your increase rounds from shifting over time and warping the piece.
Round 14	Sc 2, trp inc, sc 10, trp inc, sc 8 (26 st)
Round 15	Sc 3, trp inc, sc 12, trp inc, sc 9 (30 st)
Round 16	Sc 4, trp inc, sc 14, trp inc, sc 10 (34 st)
Round 17	Sc 5, trp inc, sc 16, trp inc, sc 11 (38 st)
Round 18	Sc 6, trp inc, sc 18, trp inc, sc 12 (42 st)
Round 19-20	Sc 42 (42 st per round) (2 rounds)
Round 21	Sc 6 (6 st) *This is not a full round, it is to adjust the position of the yarn tail for sewing*
Finishing Off	Slst to next st, cut and tie off, leaving long tail for sewing. Flatten the tail opening, then sew it closed using whip stitch sewing technique.

BODY

Use **body color** yarn. You will be starting by making two pieces, working them together, and then crocheting them together in a single round. Stuff the piece as you go.

Piece 1	
Row 1	Ch 9, starting in 2nd ch from hook: sc 8, ch 1 and turn (8 st)
Row 2	Inc, sc 6, inc, ch 1 and turn (10 st)
*Round 3	Inc, sc 8, trp inc, continue down the side of your work: sc 1, continue in the bottom of Row 1: inc, sc 6, inc, continue up the side of your work: sc 2 *The top edge should have 12 stitches; these are the only ones that you will be working into in the joining round*
Finishing Off	Cut and tie off, weave in end.

Piece 2	
Row 1	Ch 9, starting in 2nd ch from hook: sc 8, ch 1 and turn (8 st)
Row 2	Inc, sc 6, inc, ch 1 and turn (10 st)
*Round 3	Inc, sc 8, trp inc, continue down the side of your work: sc 1, continue in the bottom of Row 1: inc, sc 6, inc, continue up the side of your work: sc 2 *The top edge should have 12 stitches; these are the only ones that you will be working into in the joining round*
Round 4 (Joining Round)	Start in the first stitch of Round 3: sc 12, continue in the first available stitch of Round 3 of Piece 1: sc 11, dec (12 st)
Round 5	Starting in the first stitch of Round 4: sc 24 around (24 st)
Technique Note	From this point on, work all regular sc rounds (i.e. not bpsc rounds) in **Front Loops Only** to keep the join seam from twisting around the piece.

Round 6	Sc 24, invisible join to first stitch of the round, ch 1 (24 st)
Round 7	Start in the same stitch you just joined to: sc 24, invisible join to first st, ch 1 (24 st)
Round 8	Bpsc 24, invisible join to first st, ch 1 (24 st)
Round 9-11	Sc 24, invisible join to first st, ch 1 (24 st per round) (3 rounds)
Round 12	Bpsc 24, invisible join to first st, ch 1 (24 st)
Round 13-15	Sc 24, invisible join to first st, ch 1 (24 st per round) (3 rounds)
Round 16	Bpsc 24, invisible join to first st, ch 1 (24 st)
Round 17-19	Sc 24, invisible join to first st, ch 1 (24 st per round) (3 rounds)
Round 20	Bpsc 24, invisible join to first st, ch 1 (24 st)
Round 21-23	Sc 24, invisible join to first st, ch 1 (24 st per round) (3 rounds)
Round 24	Bpsc 24, invisible join to first st, ch 1 (24 st)
Round 25-27	Sc 24, invisible join to first st, ch 1 (24 st per round) (3 rounds)
Round 28	Bpsc 24, invisible join to first st, ch 1 (24 st)
Round 29-31	Sc 24, invisible join to first st, ch 1 (24 st per round) (3 rounds)
Round 32	Bpsc 24, invisible join to first st, ch 1 (24 st)
Round 33-35	Sc 24, invisible join to first st, ch 1 (24 st per round) (3 rounds)
Round 36	Bpsc 24, invisible join to first st, ch 1 (24 st)
Round 37-39	Sc 24, invisible join to first st, ch 1 (24 st per round) (3 rounds)
Round 40	Bpsc 24, invisible join to first st, ch 1 (24 st)
Round 41	[Sc 2, dec] 6x, invisible join to first st, ch 1 (18 st)
Round 42-43	Sc 18, invisible join to first st, ch 1 (18 st per round) (2 rounds)
Round 44	Bpsc 18, invisible join to first st, ch 1 (18 st)
Round 45-47	Sc 18, invisible join to first st, ch 1 (18 st per round) (3 rounds)
Round 48	Bpsc 18, invisible join to first st, ch 1 (18 st)
Round 49	[Sc 1, dec] 6x, invisible join to first st, ch 1 (12 st)
Round 50	Sc 12, invisible join to first st, ch 1 (12 st)
Round 51	Sc 12, slst to first st (12 st)
Finishing Off	Cut and tie off, leaving long tail for sewing. Then, flatten the opening so that the point of the V-shaped inward cut of the other end of the piece is centered with the center of the flattened opening. Use whip stitch sewing technique to sew the Round 51 end shut in a flat line.

END RESULT

ASSEMBLY

Joining Head to Back Plate

Take the Round 1 side of the Back Plate and fit the very tip of the Back Plate into the opening left on the Head piece, as shown below. Only about a round or two of the body will fit inside this hole.

Then, cut a piece of **tan** yarn and use <u>invisible sewing technique</u> all the way around where the two pieces meet to secure them together. Make sure that when you work on the bottom of the head piece, you make sure to preserve that curved shape. This will make the opening of the body segment fit properly around it.

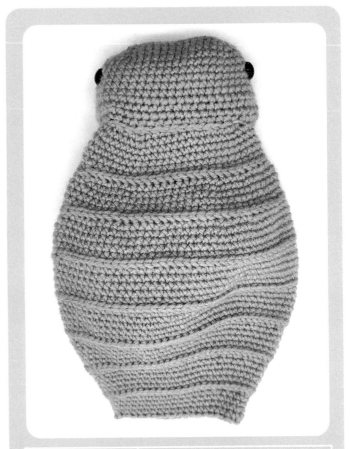

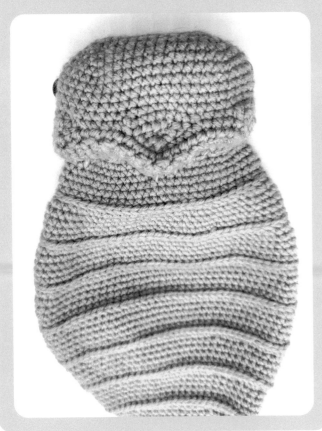

Joining Tail to Back Plate

Center the Tail along the back edge of the Back Plate and overlap the two pieces by one round.

Then, take the sewing tail from the tail and use <u>invisible sewing technique</u> to sew through both layers of the Tail and the layer of the Back Plate that makes contact with the tail. Don't go through the top layer of the Back Plate, or your seam will show.

Then, cut a very long piece of **body** yarn and sew the entire thing down wherever the body makes contact with the Head, Back Plate, and Tail pieces using seamless sewing technique, working through only the layer of the Back Plate that is touching the Body, don't work through the other side or your seam will show.

Joining Body to Entire Piece cont.

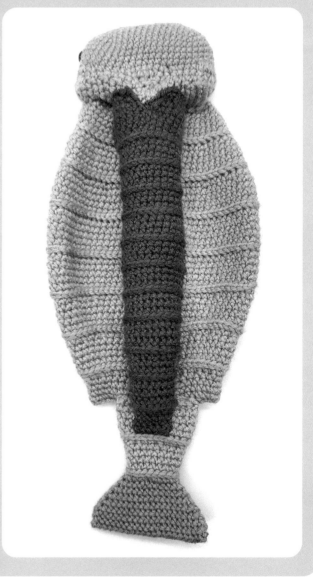

Joining Body to Entire Piece

Place the open end of the Body piece over the curved hump of the bottom of the Head piece, as shown below. Make sure the seam side is facing down so that the finished product looks smoother.

LEG PIECES (MAKE 2)

Use **leg color** yarn. You will be making 9 individual legs for each side (a total of 18 legs), and you will be crocheting each set together in numerical order into a single piece to make sewing the whole piece to the body easier.

Leg 1	
Round 1	Ch 2, sc 6 in 2nd ch from hook (6 st)
Round 2-9	Sc 6 (6 st per round) (8 rounds)
Finishing Off	Cut and tie off, weave in end.

END RESULT

Legs 2 & 8	Make 2
Round 1	Ch 2, sc 6 in 2nd ch from hook (6 st)
Round 2-11	Sc 6 (6 st per round) (10 rounds)
Finishing Off	Cut and tie off, weave in end.

END RESULT

Legs 3 & 7	Make 2
Round 1	Ch 2, sc 6 in 2nd ch from hook (6 st)
Round 2-13	Sc 6 (6 st per round) (12 rounds)
Finishing Off	Cut and tie off, weave in end.

END RESULT

Legs 4-6	Make 3
Round 1	Ch 2, sc 6 in 2nd ch from hook (6 st)
Round 2-15	Sc 6 (6 st per round) (14 rounds)
Finishing Off	Cut and tie off, weave in end.

END RESULT

Leg 9	
Round 1	Ch 2, sc 6 in 2nd ch from hook (6 st)
Round 2-9	Sc 6 (6 st per round) (8 rounds)

Round 10 (Joining Round)	Sc 3, ch 1, Grab Leg 8 and continue in the first available stitch: sc 3, ch 1 Grab Leg 7 and continue in the first available stitch: sc 3, ch 1 Grab Leg 6 and continue in the first available stitch: sc 3, ch 1 Grab Leg 5 and continue in the first available stitch: sc 3, ch 1 Grab Leg 4 and continue in the first available stitch: sc 3, ch 1 Grab Leg 3 and continue in the first available stitch: sc 3, ch 1 Grab Leg 2 and continue in the first available stitch: sc 3, ch 1 Grab Leg 1 and continue in the first available stitch: sc 6, [Sc 1 in the back of the chain in between the legs, sc 3 in the next leg starting in the first available stitch] 8x (70 st)
Finishing Off	Cut and tie off, leaving long tail for sewing.

END RESULT

ATTACHING LEGS TO BODY

Stem Wire (Optional)	If you want your legs to be poseable, insert a piece of stem wire into each leg with about half an inch sticking out. You will then push the tip of the exposed stem wire into a stitch of the body to strengthen the joint.
Alignment	Place the open end of the legs against the body so that one leg is in the center of each segment of the body with the exception of the last three towards the tail.
Sewing	Use seamless sewing technique.

77

ANTENNAE (MAKE 2)

Use **body color** yarn. If you want your antennae to be poseable and sturdy, you will add stem wire.

Round 1	Ch 2, sc 4 in 2nd ch from hook (4 st)
Round 2-21	BLO: Sc 4 (4 st per round) (20 rounds)
Finishing Off	Slst to next st, cut and tie off, leaving long tail for sewing.

END RESULT

Finishing Off	Insert a piece of stem wire into the antenna and leave about half an inch of excess sticking out of the end. I recommend tightly wrapping the exposed end with Scotch tape, it will make insertion easier later on.

END RESULT

ATTACHING ANTENNAE TO BODY

Alignment	Place the opening of the antennae two stitches back from the eyes and push the stem wire into the body there.
Sewing	Use seamless sewing technique.

FINAL PRODUCT

Your Sidneyia is officially complete! Check out the gallery below to make sure your piece came out as intended.

GALLERY

OPABINIA
(Ope-uh-BIN-ee-uh)

MATERIALS

2.5 mm Crochet Hook (or hook size of your choice)
Yarn (All Worsted Weight):

Main Color	About 1/2 of a 364 yd skein
Mouth Color	Less than 1/4 of a 364 yd skein
Tip Color	Less than 1/4 of a 364 yd skein

Stuffing
One Pair of 12 mm Safety Eyes & three 8 mm Safety Eyes
Stem Wire
Darning Needle
Stitch Marker
Sewing Pins

WHAT WAS OPABINIA?

Opabinia was a five-eyed stem group (meaning a precursor to) arthropod unlike anything else seen in this period. It was only about 2.5 inches (7 cm) in length, so this project will be a jumbo-sized version of this lovable creature.

Its name comes from the Opabin Pass between Mount Hungabee and Mount Biddle in British Columbia, Canada near the Burgess Shale where it was discovered.

When Harry B. Whittington, a paleontologist who wrote extensively on Opabinia, first presented the creature to an audience, everyone laughed!

Opabinia's most stand-out feature, its long proboscis, was not its actual mouth as is commonly assumed. Instead, it was more like an arm that was used to grab food and feed it back to its actual mouth behind the appendage.

Though often depicted in media as grasping at live prey, scientists believe that Opabinia likely used its proboscis to root around in the dirt on the sea floor looking for particles of food rather than actively hunting. It also lacked a jaw capable of crushing up larger prey as well.

Despite being an arthropod with a shell, it was actually soft-bodied, at least by arthropod standards. It still had a shell, but this shell was soft enough to be flexible, giving it added maneuverability. If you have ever peeled raw shrimp before, you have felt this type of shell.

Opabinia is so unusual that it led Whittington to assert that many Cambrian creatures cannot be classified into modern groups and should not be forced into them!

Finished Size:
Approx. 20 in
(51 cm) long
from mouth to tail,
Results may vary
depending on
individual tension.

DIFFICULTY:

ADVANCED INTERMEDIATE

*This pattern is
a bit tedious,
but the result is
well worth it!

BODY SEGMENT HALF PIECE 1 (MAKE 4)

Use **tip color** yarn; you will switch to **mouth color** and then **main color** when prompted to do so. Do not stuff the tips.

Round 1	Ch 2, sc 4 in 2nd ch from hook (4 st)
Round 2	Inc 2, sc 2 (6 st)
Round 3	Sc 6 (6 st)
Round 4	Inc 3, sc 3 (9 st)
Round 5	Sc 9 (9 st)
Round 6	[Sc 1, inc] 3x, sc 3 (12 st)
Round 7-8	Sc 12 (12 st per round) (2 rounds)
Color Change	Switch to **mouth color** yarn.
Round 9	Slst, sc 11 (12 st) *Starting the first round of a new color with a slst will make the color transition smoother; you will work into the slst in the next round like a normal sc stitch*
Round 10-11	Sc 12 (12 st per round) (2 rounds)
Color Change	Switch to **main color** yarn.
Round 12	Slst, sc 11 (12 st)
Round 13	Sc 12 (12 st)
*Row 14	Sc 7, ch 1 and turn (7 st)
Row 15-23	Sc 6, ch 1 and turn (6 st per row) (9 rows)
*Round 24	Sc 6, continue down the side of your work (working 1 sc into the side of each row): sc 10, drop down to unworked stitches of the round below: sc 6, continue up the side of the rows: sc 8, inc (32 st)

Finishing Off	Slst to first stitch of Round 24, cut and tie off, leaving long tail for sewing.

END RESULT

BODY SEGMENT HALF PIECE 2 (MAKE 4)

Use **tip color** yarn; you will switch to **mouth color** and then **main color** when prompted to do so. Do not stuff the tips.

Round 1	Ch 2, sc 4 in 2nd ch from hook (4 st)
Round 2	Inc 2, sc 2 (6 st)
Round 3	Sc 6 (6 st)
Round 4	Inc 3, sc 3 (9 st)
Round 5	Sc 9 (9 st)
Round 6	[Sc 1, inc] 3x, sc 3 (12 st)
Round 7-8	Sc 12 (12 st per round) (2 rounds)

Color Change	Switch to **mouth color** yarn.
Round 9	Slst, sc 11 (12 st) *Starting the first round of a new color with a slst will make the color transition smoother; you will work into the slst in the next round like a normal sc stitch*
Round 10-11	Sc 12 (12 st per round) (2 rounds)
Color Change	Switch to **main color** yarn.
Round 12	Slst, sc 11 (12 st)
Round 13-16	Sc 12 (12 st per round) (4 rounds)
*Row 17-26	Sc 6, ch 1 and turn (6 st per row) (10 rows)
*Round 27	Sc 6, continue down the side of your work (working 1 sc into the side of each row): sc 10, drop down to unworked stitches of the round below: sc 6, continue up the side of the rows: sc 8, inc (32 st)
Finishing Off	Slst to first stitch of Round 27, cut and tie off, leaving long tail for sewing.

END RESULT

BODY SEGMENT HALF PIECE 3 (MAKE 6)

Use **tip color** yarn; you will switch to **mouth color** and then **main color** when prompted to do so. Do not stuff the tips.

Round 1	Ch 2, sc 4 in 2nd ch from hook (4 st)
Round 2	Inc 2, sc 2 (6 st)
Round 3	Sc 6 (6 st)
Round 4	Inc 3, sc 3 (9 st)
Round 5	Sc 9 (9 st)
Round 6	[Sc 1, inc] 3x, sc 3 (12 st)
Round 7-8	Sc 12 (12 st per round) (2 rounds)

Color Change	Switch to **mouth color** yarn.
Round 9	Slst, sc 11 (12 st) *Starting the first round of a new color with a slst will make the color transition smoother; you will work into the slst in the next round like a normal sc stitch*
Round 10-11	Sc 12 (12 st per round) (2 rounds)
Color Change	Switch to **main color** yarn.
Round 12	Slst, sc 11 (12 st)
Round 13-19	Sc 12 (12 st per round) (7 rounds)
*Row 20-29	Sc 6, ch 1 and turn (6 st per row) (10 rows)
*Round 30	Sc 6, continue down the side of your work (working 1 sc into the side of each row): sc 10, drop down to unworked stitches of the round below: sc 6, continue up the side of the rows: sc 8, inc (32 st)
Finishing Off	Slst to first stitch of Round 30, cut and tie off, leaving long tail for sewing.

END RESULT

BODY SEGMENT HALF PIECE 4 (MAKE 2)

Use **mouth color** yarn; you will switch to **main color** when prompted to do so. Do not stuff the tips.

Round 1	Ch 2, sc 4 in 2nd ch from hook (4 st)
Round 2	Inc 2, sc 2 (6 st)
Round 3	Sc 6 (6 st)
Round 4	Inc 3, sc 3 (9 st)
Round 5	Sc 9 (9 st)
Round 6	[Sc 1, inc] 3x, sc 3 (12 st)

Round 7-8	Sc 12 (12 st per round) (2 rounds)
Color Change	Switch to **mouth color** yarn.
Round 9	Slst, sc 11 (12 st)
Round 10	Sc 12 (12 st)
*Row 11-20	Sc 6, ch 1 and turn (6 st per row) (10 rows)
*Round 21	Sc 6, continue down the side of your work (working 1 sc into the side of each row): sc 10, drop down to unworked stitches of the round below: sc 6, continue up the side of the rows: sc 8, inc (32 st)
Finishing Off	Slst to first stitch of Round 21, cut and tie off, leaving long tail for sewing.

END RESULT

BODY SEGMENT HALF PIECE 5 (MAKE 2)

Use **main color** yarn. Do not stuff the tips.

Round 1	Ch 2, sc 4 in 2nd ch from hook (4 st)
Round 2	Inc 2, sc 2 (6 st)
Round 3	Sc 6 (6 st)
Round 4	Inc 3, sc 3 (9 st)
Round 5	Sc 9 (9 st)
Round 6	[Sc 1, inc] 3x, sc 3 (12 st)
Round 7	Sc 12, ch 1 and turn (12 st)
Row 8-17	Sc 6, ch 1 and turn (6 st per row) (10 rows)
*Round 18	Sc 6, continue down the side of your work (working 1 sc into the side of each row): sc 10, drop down to unworked stitches of the round below: sc 6, continue up the side of the rows: sc 8, inc (32 st)
Finishing Off	Slst to first stitch of Round 18, cut and tie off, leaving long tail for sewing.

END RESULT

END RESULT

BODY SEGMENT HALF PIECE 6 (MAKE 2)

Use **main color** yarn. Do not stuff the tips.

Row 1	Ch 7, starting in 2nd ch from hook, sc 6 across, ch 1 and turn (6 st)
Row 2-9	Sc 6, ch 1 and turn (9 st per row) (8 rows)
*Round 10	Sc 6, continue down the side of your work (working 1 sc into the side of each row): sc 9, inc, continue along the bottom of the piece: sc 5, inc, continue up the side of the rows: sc 9, inc (35 st)
Finishing Off	Slst to first stitch of Round 10, cut and tie off, leaving long tail for sewing.

ASSEMBLING BODY SEGMENT PIECE PAIRS 1-5

Alignment	Align the top edge of the flat pieces with the bottom of the opening on the other body segment piece, so that the pieces fit together yin and yang style. Make sure that each of these pairs are of the same kind (i.e. Body Segment Half Piece 1s are paired with other 1s, etc.) You need to also make sure that the slanted end of the tips of each piece are facing the same way as well.

Sewing	Use <u>whip stitch sewing technique</u> to sew just the edge, leaving the sides of the flat pieces open. Don't get rid of your sewing tails just yet, you'll need them to sew the completed body segments to each other in the next step. The tails in the photo are simply tucked inside the pieces.

ASSEMBLING BODY SEGMENT 6 PIECES

Alignment	Place the two pieces against each other with the right sides facing out (right side is relative to the Round 10 border of the pieces)
Sewing	Use <u>invisible sewing technique</u> on the short ends, leaving the long ends open. Leave your sewing ends for now, you will use them to sew together the completed body segments.

CONNECTING ASSEMBLED BODY SEGMENTS TO EACH OTHER

Order of Body Segments	1-2-3-3-3-2-1-4-5-6
Alignment	In the order defined above, line up the center holes of each body segment piece with the slanted side of the tips pointing towards the front of the animal
Sewing	Use <u>zig zag sewing technique</u> around the center holes of the segment pieces to preserve the edge of each segment. As you go, thread the stem wire through if desired and stuff the center of the segments.

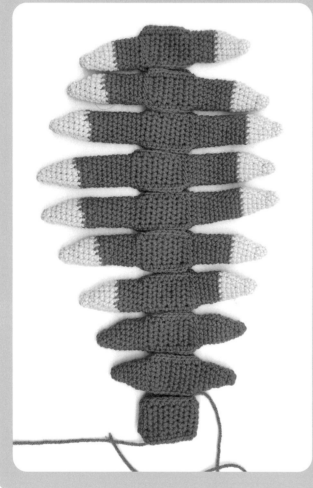

Sewing Pt. 2

Once all of the body segments are joined, cut a very long piece of **main color** yarn and use <u>whip stitch sewing technique</u> to sew the loose-hanging segments to each other along the edges so that they come together into one whole flat piece. You will sew up until you reach the highest of the two **mouth color/tip color** edges and leave the rest hanging free.

The only yarn tail left unwoven should be the one hanging off of the Body Segment 6, which will be used to sew on the tail. You will also want to have about 6 inches (15 cm) of stem wire still sticking out of the head side of the body.

Row 2	FLO: Slst 2, ch 2, dc 6, hdc 6, sc 7, trp inc, sc 7, hdc 7, dc 7, ch 1 and turn (45 st) *End of row stitch count will not include any of the chain stitches*
Row 3	BLO: Slst 2, ch 2, dc 6, hdc 7, sc 7, trp inc, sc 7, hdc 7, dc 5, ch 1 and turn (44 st)
Row 4	FLO: Slst 2, ch 2, dc 5, hdc 6, sc 7, trp inc, sc 7, hdc 6, dc 6, ch 1 and turn (42 st)
Color Change	Switch to **mouth color** yarn.
Row 5	BLO: Slst 2, ch 2, dc 5, hdc 6, sc 7, trp inc, sc 7, hdc 6, dc 4, ch 1 and turn (40 st)
Row 6	FLO: Slst 2, ch 2, dc 5, hdc 6, sc 5, trp inc, sc 6, hdc 6, dc 5 (38 st)
Finishing Off	Cut and tie off, weave in all ends.

TAIL

Start with **main color** yarn. You will switch to **mouth color** yarn when prompted.

Note: hdc stitches technically have three loops to them. When you work BLO or FLO into an hdc stitch, make sure you include the middle of those three loops as well as the front or back loop

Row 1	Ch 25, starting in 3rd ch from hook, dc 7, hdc 7, sc 8, inc, continue along the bottom of the chains starting in the bottom of the inc you just made: sc 8, hdc 7, dc 6, ch 1 and turn (45 st)

END RESULT

ATTACHING TAIL

Alignment	Push the round end of the tail into the Body Segment 6 hole as far as you can without it bunching up.
Sewing	Use the tail from Body Segment 6 and use zig zag sewing technique, going through both layers of the Body Segment 6 piece as well as through the tail. Weave in ends.

HEAD

Use **main color** yarn. You will stuff this piece later.

Round 1	Ch 6, starting in 2nd ch from hook, sc 4, inc, continue on bottom of your work starting in the bottom of the inc you just made: sc 4, inc (12 st)
Round 2	Inc, sc 3, inc 3, sc 3, inc 2 (18 st)
Round 3	Sc 1, inc, sc 3, [sc 1, inc] 3x, sc 3, [sc 1, inc] 2x (24 st)
Round 4-9	Sc 24 (24 st per round) (6 rounds)
Finishing Off	Slst to next st, cut and tie off, leaving long tail for sewing.

END RESULT

EYE STALKS (MAKE 5)

Use **main color** yarn. No need to stuff these pieces.

Round 1	Ch 2, sc 6 in 2nd ch from hook (6 st)
Round 2-3	Sc 6 (6 st per round) (2 rounds)
Safety Eyes	Place your safety eye in the center of Round 1. Two will be 12 mm and three will be 8 mm.
Round 4-5	Sc 6 (6 st per round) (2 rounds)
Finishing Off	Slst to next st, cut and tie off, leaving long tail for sewing.

ATTACHING EYE STALKS

Alignment	There will be three eyes on the top and two eyes on the bottom, towards the closed part of the head. The two big eyes will be the top two outer eyes.
Sewing	Use whip stitch sewing technique to sew the stalks onto the top of the head.

END RESULT

ATTACHING HEAD

Alignment	Put the hole of the head over the remaining body hole, making sure that the eyes are facing the same direction as the ribbed side of the tail. If you are using stem wire, thread the piece between rounds 5 and 6 on the bottom side of the head, centered horizontally.
Sewing	Use zig zag sewing technique to sew the head to the front opening of the body. Stuff the head before sealing it off completely.

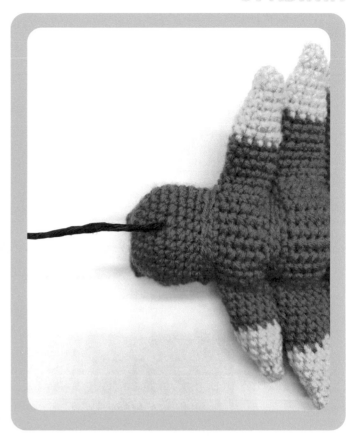

MOUTH TUBE

Use **mouth color** yarn. If you are using stem wire, do not stuff. If not, you may want to add a small amount of stuffing to help it keep its shape.

When making your slipknot, be sure to leave a long tail to make sewing easier

Round 1	Ch 10, starting in furthest ch from hook, sc 10 around (10 st)
Round 2-3	Sc 10 (10 st per round) (2 rounds)
Round 4	Slst 4, sc 6 (10 st)
Round 5	Ddslst 4, sc 6 (10 st)
Round 6	Ddsc 4, sc 6 (10 st)
Round 7	Sc 10 (10 st)
Round 8	Slst 4, sc 6 (10 st)
Round 9	Ddslst 4, sc 6 (10 st)

Round 10	Ddsc 4, sc 6 (10 st)
Round 11	Sc 11 (11 st) *This round goes 1 st past a full round to correct alignment*
Round 12	Slst 4, sc 6 (10 st)
Round 13	Ddslst 4, sc 6 (10 st)
Round 14	Ddsc 4, sc 6 (10 st)
Round 15-17	Sc 10 (10 st per round) (3 rounds)
Finishing Off	Slst to next st, cut and tie off, leaving long tail for sewing

END RESULT

MOUTH

Use **mouth color** yarn.

Round 1	Ch 17, starting in 2nd ch from hook, sc 15, inc, continue on bottom starting in the bottom of the inc stitch: sc 15, {sc, ch 1, dc, ch 1} (34 st, not counting two ch stitches)

Terminology Note	Note that there are curly brackets { } in the next round. These indicate that everything within them will be done in the same stitch.
Round 2	Inc, [ch 2, starting in 2nd ch from hook: slst, sc in next available st] 5x, trp dec, [ch 2, starting in 2nd ch from hook: slst, sc 1 in next available st] 6x, inc, {sc 1, ch 1, dc, ch 1}, inc, sc 1, [ch 2, starting in 2nd ch from hook: slst, sc 1 in next available st] 6x, trp dec, [ch 2, starting in 2nd ch from hook: slst, sc in next available st] 5x, inc, {sc 1, ch 1, dc, ch 1}
Finishing Off	Slst to the chain space that came after the dc stitch from Round 1, cut and tie off, weave in end.

END RESULT

CONNECTING MOUTH TO MOUTH TUBE

Alignment	Place the mouth piece over the tube so that when the L-shaped tube is sitting vertically upright, the top and bottom "jaws" of the mouth are horizontal.
Sewing	You will use <u>whip stitch sewing technique</u> to secure the tube to the mouth. Make a few stitches to get the mouth somewhat secured into place, and then use your finger or the back of your crochet hook to push the center of the mouth down into the tube just a bit. This will help make the mouth close a bit. Finish sewing with the mouth in this position.

Closing Mouth	Using a **mouth color** piece of yarn, sew the mouth closed just at the tips of the jaws.

CONNECTING MOUTH TUBE TO HEAD

Alignment	Align the tube so that the front edge is 2-3 rows back from the center of where the head piece started. If you used stem wire, simply pull the mouth tube over the exposed wire and position it where the wire lies. If your wire is too long, cut it to fit and bend the end over itself so that there is no sharp end that can poke through.
Sewing	Use seamless sewing technique.

FINAL PRODUCT

Your Opabinia is officially complete! Check out the gallery on the next page to make sure your piece came out as intended.

GALLERY

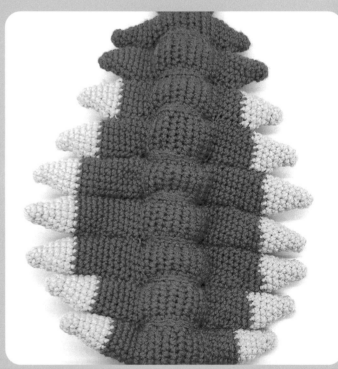

WIWAXIA
(Wih-WAX-ee-uh)

MATERIALS

2.5 mm Crochet Hook (or hook size of your choice)
Yarn (All Worsted Weight):

Shell Color	Less than 1/2 of a 364 yd skein
Foot Color	Less than 1/4 of a 364 yd skein
Spine Color	Less than 1/4 of a 364 yd skein
Leg Color	Only a few yards

Stuffing
Darning Needle
Stitch Marker
Sewing Pins

WHAT WAS WIWAXIA?

Wiwaxia was an ancient mollusk-like creature that existed from the Middle Cambrian up until the middle of the Ordovician period that came after (520-465 MYA).

These unusual little guys were only about 2 inches (5 cm) long when fully grown. Paleontologists have found baby specimens that are as small as 2 mm long! Upon its discovery, there was debate over whether or not Wiwaxia was part of the annelid group (segmented worms), but the current evidence places them in the mollusk category.

From the hundreds of specimens we have from the Burgess Shale, it would seem that Wiwaxias were lone wolves rather than grouping up together with others of their species.

Wiwaxia's most standout feature is certainly its unusual armor. Each of these leaf-shaped pieces is called a "sclerite", and they were rooted in the skin of the creature the same way hair and feathers are. They were all separately attached to Wiwaxia, which implies that its structure was likely flexible. They were not hard like rock, they were strong but flexible, made of a carbon-based polymer material.

The spines on its back were most likely used for defense against predators. They were regenerative, meaning that if a Wiwaxia broke off one of its spines, the spine would grow back.

Most of the bottom side of the Wiwaxia was taken up by a slug-like foot that it used to move around the sea floor like a snail. Its mouth consisted of two to three rows of teeth, which it used to scrape at mats of bacteria on the sea floor.

Finished Size:
Approx. 6 in
(15 cm) long
and 4 inches
(10 cm) tall,
Results may vary
depending on
individual tension.

DIFFICULTY:

ADVANCED INTERMEDIATE

SHELL

Use **shell color** yarn. Note in this pattern that curly brackets { } mean that all stitches within them are done in the same stitch.

Row 1	Ch 9, dc 1 in the 3rd ch from hook, ch 2, skip 2 ch, dc 2 in the same chain, ch 2, skip 2 ch, dc 2 in the last ch (6 dc stitches, including the first 2 chains of the row)
Row 2	Ch 3, turn your work 90 degrees so that the last dc you worked is horizontal. Then, work 4 dc stitches around the post of this stitch, ch 1, rotate 180 degrees, then dc 5 around the post of the second dc stitch, ch 1, skip the next set of dc 2 from Row 1, rotate 180 degrees and work 5 dc in the post of the first available dc from Row 1, ch 1, rotate 180 degrees, and work 5 dc in the post of the last dc of Row 1 (2 crocodile stitches)
Row 3	Ch 3, dc 2 in the center of the last crocodile stitch, ch 2, work {dc 2, ch 2, dc 2} in the space between the two dc posts from Row 1 that did not have a scale worked into them, ch 2, work {dc 2, ch 2, dc 2} in the center of the next crocodile stitch (5 sets of 2 dc stitches)

Row 4	Ch 3, work a crocodile stitch into the first set of posts, ch 1, skip next set of posts and work another crocodile stitch into the set of posts after that, ch 1, work a crocodile stitch into the last set of posts (3 crocodile stitches)
Row 5	Ch 3, work {dc 2, ch 2, dc 2} in the center of the next available crocodile stitch, ch 2, dc 2 in the center of the unworked set of posts, ch 2, dc 2 in the center of the next crocodile stitch, ch 2, dc 2 in the center of the next unworked set of posts, ch 2, work {dc 2, ch 2, dc 2} in the center of the last crocodile stitch (7 sets of 2 dc stitches)
Row 6	Ch 3, [work a crocodile stitch into the next available set of posts, ch 1, skip the next set of posts] 3x, work a crocodile stitch into the last available set of posts (4 crocodile stitches)
Row 7	Ch 3, [dc 2 in center of first crocodile stitch, ch 2, dc 2 in the center of the next available unworked set of posts, ch 2] 3x, dc 2 in the center of the last crocodile stitch (7 sets of 2 dc stitches)
Row 8	Ch 3, [crocodile stitch, ch 1, skip next set of posts] 3x, crocodile stitch in last set of posts (4 crocodile stitches)

Row 9-18	Repeat the Row 7 and 8 sequence 5 times total for a total of 10 rounds, repeating Row 7 on odd rows and Row 8 on even rows. (You should have a total of 7 rows of 4 crocodile stitches)
Row 19	Ch 3, dc 2 in the center of the first crocodile stitch, ch 2, make a dc dec in the center of the next set of unworked posts and in the center of the crocodile stitch that comes after it, ch 2, dc 2 in the center of the next set of unworked posts, ch 2, make a dc dec in the center of the next crocodile stitch and in the center of the next set of unworked posts after it, ch 2, dc 2 in the center of the last crocodile stitch (5 sets of 2 dc stitches, treating the two dc dec the same as a normal set of 2 dc)
Row 20	Ch 3, [crocodile stitch, ch 1, skip next set of posts] 2x, crocodile stitch in the last set of posts (3 crocodile stitches)
Row 21	Ch 3, dc dec in the center of the first crocodile stitch and in the center of the next set of unworked posts, ch 2, dc 2 in the center of the next crocodile stitch, ch 2, dc dec in the center of the next set of unworked posts and in the center of the last crocodile stitch (3 sets of 2 dc, treating the two dc dec the same as a normal set of 2 dc)

Row 22	Ch 3, work a crocodile stitch in the dc dec the same way you would a regular set of dc, ch 2, skip next set of posts, crocodile stitch into the last dc dec set (2 crocodile stitches)
Finishing Off	Slip stitch to the ch 3 part from the beginning of Row 22, cut and tie off, leaving long tail for sewing

END RESULT

BODY

Use **shell color** yarn. Do not stuff this piece.

Round 1	Ch 6, starting in 2nd ch from hook: sc 4, inc, continue in the bottom of your stitches starting with the one you just made your inc stitch into: sc 4, inc (12 st)
Important Technique Note	From this point on, work in Front Loops Only. This will greatly reduce the amount of shifting that happens in your stitches over time and will keep your increases straight and square.
Round 2	Sc 2, inc, sc 2, trp inc, sc 5, trp inc (17 st)
Round 3	Sc 2, 2/3 inc, sc 3, trp inc, sc 7, trp inc, sc 1 (22 st)
Round 4	Sc 3, inc, sc 5, trp inc, sc 9, trp inc, sc 2 (27 st)
Round 5	Sc 3, 2/3 inc, sc 6, trp inc, sc 11, trp inc, sc 3 (32 st)
Round 6	Sc 4, inc, sc 8, trp inc, sc 13, trp inc, sc 4 (37 st)
Round 7	Sc 4, 2/3 inc, sc 9, trp inc, sc 15, trp inc, sc 5 (42 st)
Round 8-21	Sc 42 (42 st per round) (14 rounds)
Round 22	Sc 5, 2/3 dec, sc 9, trp dec, sc 15, trp dec, sc 5 (37 st in round, 38 st total) *This round goes 1 st past a full round to adjust alignment*
Round 23	Sc 4, dec, sc 8, trp dec, sc 13, trp dec, sc 4 (32 st)
Round 24	Sc 3, 2/3 dec, sc 6, trp dec, sc 11, trp dec, sc 3 (27 st)
Round 25	Sc 3, dec, sc 5, trp dec, sc 9, trp dec, sc 2 (22 st)
Round 26	Sc 2, 2/3 dec, sc 3, trp dec, sc 7, trp dec, sc 1 (17 st)
Round 27	Sc 2, dec, sc 2, trp dec, sc 5, trp dec (12 st)
Finishing Off	Slst to next st, cut and tie off, leaving long tail for sewing, use your tail to sew the remaining hole shut horizontally (along the same axis as your Round 1) with a whip stitch sewing technique in the front loops. Flatten the piece so that it is concaved.

END RESULT

Round 4	Sc 2, inc, sc 3, [sc 2, inc] 3x, sc 3, [sc 2, inc] 2x (30 st)
Round 5	Sc 3, inc, sc 3, [sc 3, inc] 3x, sc 3, [sc 3, inc] 2x (36 st)
Round 6	Sc 4, inc, sc 3, [sc 4, inc] 3x, sc 3, [sc 4, inc] 2x (42 st)
Round 7	Sc 5, inc, sc 3, [sc 5, inc] 3x, sc 3, [sc 5, inc] 2x (48 st)
Round 8	Sc 48 (48 st)
Round 9	Sc 5, dec, sc 3, [sc 5, dec] 3x, sc 3, [sc 5, dec] 2x (42 st)
Round 10	Sc 4, dec, sc 3, [sc 4, dec] 3x, sc 3, [sc 4, dec] 2x (36 st)
Color Change	Switch to **leg color** yarn.
Round 11	Sc 5, [Ch 5, starting in 2nd st from hook: slst 4, return to round: sc 2] 14x, sc 3 (14 tentacles and 36 st between)
Finishing Off	Slst to next st, cut and tie off, leaving long tail for sewing

FOOT

Start with **foot color** yarn. You will switch to **leg color** yarn towards the end to make little legs. This piece will be very lightly stuffed during assembly.

Round 1	Ch 6, starting in 2nd ch from hook: sc 4, inc, continue in the bottom of your stitches starting with the one you just made your inc stitch into: sc 4, inc (12 st)
Round 2	Inc, sc 3, inc 3, sc 3, inc 2 (18 st)
Round 3	Sc 1, inc, sc 3, [sc 1, inc] 3x, sc 3, [sc 1, inc] 2x (24 st)

END RESULT

END RESULT

SPIKES (MAKE 2)

Use **spike color** yarn. You will be making 6 spikes per side for a total of 12 spikes.

Round 1	Ch 2, sc 4 in 2nd ch from hook (4 st)
Round 2-7	Sc 4 (4 st per round) (6 rounds)
Round 8	[Sc 1, inc] 2x (6 st)
Round 9-14	Sc 6 (6 st per round) (6 rounds)
Round 15	[Sc 2, inc] 2x (8 st)
Round 16-21	Sc 8 (8 st per round) (6 rounds)
Finishing Off	Cut and tie off, weave in end

MOUTH

Use **foot color** yarn.

Round 1	Ch 2, sc 6 in 2nd ch from hook (6 st)
Round 2	Inc 6 (12 st)
Round 3	Bpsc 12 (12 st)
Round 4	[Sc 1, inc] 6x (18 st)
Finishing Off	Slst to next st, cut and tie off, leaving long tail for sewing

END RESULT

END RESULT

ASSEMBLING SHELL AND SPIKES

Inserting Spikes	In the Shell piece, there are gaps in between the crocodile stitches, as shown by the blue crochet hook end in the photo below. You will be pulling all of your spikes through these gaps. Place 6 on each side with 2 crocodile stitches between them in the middle. The Row 22 side of the shell should be the front, and there will be 3 rows of crocodile stitches that go past the spikes, while the back side will only have two rows of crocodile stitches before the spikes begin. On the bottom side, the opening of the spikes should be flush against the bottom of the shell.

Sewing	Cut a long piece of **shell color** yarn. Then, use <u>whip stitch sewing technique</u> to go around the openings of each spike and secure it to the shell.

ASSEMBLING BODY PIECES

Attaching Mouth to Body	Place the mouth piece onto the inside of the concaved body piece with the top edge of the mouth about 2 rounds back from the very tip of the body. I recommend treating the Round 1 end of the body as the head since it looks smoother.
Sewing	Use <u>invisible sewing technique</u> to secure it. Make sure you are only going through one layer of the body and not both.

Attaching Foot to Body	Place the foot on the same side of the body as the mouth. The end with no white tentacles will be up against the mouth.
Sewing	Use <u>seamless sewing technique</u> around the edge of the foot piece where it makes contact with the body and VERY LIGHTLY stuff it before closing it off completely. The pink part of the foot should hang over the white edge of the piece and cover it up.

Attaching Shell Piece to Body Piece	Place the Shell piece over the Body piece with the head sides of each (explained previously) lined up with each other.
Sewing	Use the long tail from the shell to sew the shell onto the body using <u>invisible sewing technique</u>.

FINAL PRODUCT

Your Wiwaxia is officially complete! Check out the gallery on the next page to make sure your piece came out as intended.

GALLERY

PAMBDELURION

(Pam-duh-LURR-ee-in)

MATERIALS

2.5 mm Crochet Hook (or hook size of your choice)
Yarn (All Worsted Weight):

Back Color	About 1/2 of a 364 yd skein
Stomach Color	About 1/2 of a 364 yd skein
Accent Color	Only a few yards

Stuffing
Stem Wire
Darning Needle
Stitch Marker
Sewing Pins

WHAT WAS PAMBDELURION?

Pambdelurion was a member of the panarthropod clade, and it was surprisingly large for this time period. It could grow to about 2 feet (60 cm) in length! It's full name is *Pambdelurion Whittingtoni*, named after the paleontologist Harry B. Whittington.

As with most Cambrian creatures, it was discovered in the Burgess Shale in British Columbia, Canada. Very little is known about this creature, but it is believed to have been a predator that fed on smaller arthropod creatures.

It was a part of the Lobopodian (meaning "lobe legs") group known as the gilled-lobopodians. This means that the flipper pieces on its sides may have been gill-like structures that allowed Pambdelurion to breathe! Fun fact: the mighty tardigrade comes from the very same group as the Pambdelurion!

Since these flaps were probably used for respiration and not movement, Pambdelurion likely wasn't a very talented swimmer. It most likely crawled around on the ocean floor. The real Pambdelurion had 11 sets of these flaps, rather than the 6 featured in this pattern.

The appendages on its head were likely sensory organs that helped it to get around since it did not have eyes. It had layers of hard plates in its mouth that would shoot out into a cone shape to grasp and draw in prey.

The Pambdelurion is closely related to or potentially even in the same genus as a Cambrian creature known as the Omnidens Amplus that was discovered in China, which could reach the height of a man!

Finished Size:
Approx. 9 in
(23 cm) long
and 6 inches
(15 cm) tall,
Results may vary
depending on
individual tension.

DIFFICULTY:

ADVANCED INTERMEDIATE

BACK

Use **back color** yarn.

Row 1	Ch 2, sc 3 in 2nd ch from hook, ch 1 and turn (3 st)
Row 2	Inc 3, ch 1 and turn (6 st)
Row 3	[Sc 1, inc] 3x, ch 1 and turn (9 st)
Row 4-8	Sc 9, ch 1 and turn (9 st per row) (5 rows)
Row 9	Dec, sc 1, 2/3 dec, sc 1, dec, ch 1 and turn (6 st)
Row 10	Inc, sc 1, 2/3 inc, sc 1, inc, ch 1 and turn (9 st)
Row 11	Inc, sc 3, inc, sc 3, inc, ch 1 and turn (12 st)
Row 12-15	Sc 12, ch 1 and turn (12 st per row) (4 rows)
Row 16	Dec, sc 3, dec, sc 3, dec, ch 1 and turn (9 st)
Row 17	Inc, sc 3, inc, sc 3, inc, ch 1 and turn (12 st)
Row 18	Inc, sc 4, 2/3 inc, sc 4, inc, ch 1 and turn (15 st)
Row 19-22	Sc 15, ch 1 and turn (15 st per row) (4 rows)
Row 23	Dec, sc 4, 2/3 dec, sc 4, dec, ch 1 and turn (12 st)
Row 24	Inc, sc 4, 2/3 inc, sc 4, inc, ch 1 and turn (15 st)
Row 25	Inc, sc 6, inc, sc 6, inc, ch 1 and turn (18 st)
Row 26-29	Sc 18 (18 st per row) (4 rows)
Row 30	Dec, sc 6, dec, sc 6, dec, ch 1 and turn (15 st)
Row 31	Dec, sc 4, 2/3 dec, sc 4, dec, ch 1 and turn (12 st)
Row 32	Inc, sc 4, 2/3 inc, sc 4, inc, ch 1 and turn (15 st)
Row 33-36	Sc 15, ch 1 and turn (15 st per row) (4 rows)
Row 37	Dec, sc 4, 2/3 dec, sc 4, dec, ch 1 and turn (12 st)
Row 38	Dec, sc 3, dec, sc 3, dec, ch 1 and turn (9 st)
Row 39	Inc, sc 3, inc, sc 3, inc, ch 1 and turn (12 st)
Row 40-43	Sc 12 (12 st per row) (4 rows)
Row 44	Dec, sc 3, dec, sc 3, dec, ch 1 and turn (9 st)
Row 45	Inc, sc 3, inc, sc 3, inc, ch 1 and turn (12 st)
Row 46-50	Sc 12 (12 st per row) (5 rows)
Row 51	Dec, sc 3, dec, sc 3, dec, ch 1 and turn (9 st)
Row 52	Inc, sc 3, inc, sc 3, inc, ch 1 and turn (12 st)
Row 53-57	Sc 12 (12 st per row) (5 rows)
Row 58	[Sc 2, dec] 3x, ch 1 and turn (9 st)
Row 59	[Sc 1, dec] 3x, ch 1 and turn (6 st)
Row 60	Dec 3, ch 1 and turn (3 st)
Row 61	Trp dec, work down the side of your work (1 sc in the side of each row): sc 10, ch 1 and turn (11 st)
Row 62	Sc 8, ch 1 and turn (8 st)
Row 63	Inc, sc 7, ch 1 and turn (9 st)
Row 64	Sc 8, inc, ch 1 and turn (10 st)
Row 65-66	Sc 10, ch 1 and turn (10 st per row) (2 rows)
Row 67	Dec, sc 7, inc, ch 1 and turn (10 st)
Row 68	Inc, sc 7, dec, ch 1 and turn (10 st)
Row 69	Dec, sc 7, inc, ch 1 and turn (10 st)
Row 70	Inc, sc 7, dec, ch 1 and turn (10 st)

Row 71	Dec, sc 8, ch 1 and turn (9 st)
Row 72	Inc, sc 6, dec, ch 1 and turn (9 st)
Row 73	Dec, sc 7, ch 1 and turn (8 st)
Row 74	Inc, sc 5, dec, ch 1 and turn (8 st)
Row 75	Dec, sc 6, ch 1 and turn (7 st)
Row 76	Inc, sc 4, dec, ch 1 and turn (7 st)
Row 77	Dec, sc 5, ch 1 and turn (6 st)
Row 78	Inc, sc 3, dec, ch 1 and turn (6 st)
Row 79	Dec, sc 4, ch 1 and turn (5 st)
Row 80	Inc, sc 2, dec, ch 1 and turn (5 st)
Row 81	Dec, sc 3, ch 1 and turn (4 st)
Row 82	Inc, sc 1, dec, ch 1 and turn (4 st)
Row 83	Dec, sc 2, ch 1 and turn (3 st)
Row 84	Inc, dec, ch 1 and turn (3 st)
Row 85	Trp dec (1 st)
Finishing Off	Cut and tie off, weave in end.

END RESULT

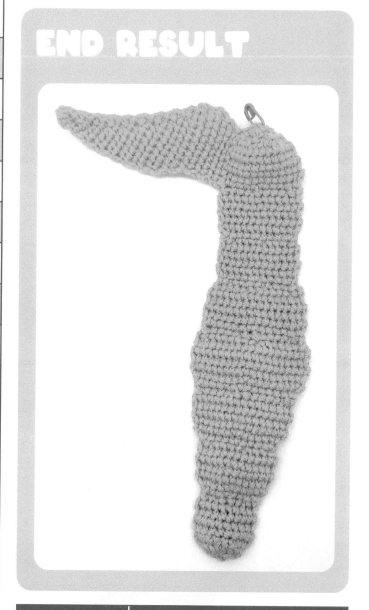

Reattaching Yarn for 2nd Head Piece	Take note of the row where your last sc of Row 61 was (this should be around the 10th row back from the tr dec of Row 61), and reattach your yarn to the side of this row. You will make your first stitch in this stitch. The rows will continue numbering at 61 so that the numbers of this piece match the numbers of the first head piece for easy reference and comparison.

Row 75	Sc 6, dec, ch 1 and turn (7 st)
Row 76	Dec, sc 4, inc, ch 1 and turn (7 st)
Row 77	Sc 5, dec, ch 1 and turn (6 st)
Row 78	Dec, sc 3, inc, ch 1 and turn (6 st)
Row 79	Sc 4, dec, ch 1 and turn (5 st)
Row 80	Dec, sc 2, inc, ch 1 and turn (5 st)
Row 81	Sc 3, dec, ch 1 and turn (4 st)
Row 82	Dec, sc, inc, ch 1 and turn (4 st)
Row 83	Sc 2, dec, ch 1 and turn (3 st)
Row 84	Dec, inc, ch 1 and turn (3 st)
*Round 85 (Border Round)	Tr dec, ch 6, starting in 2nd ch from hook: slst 5, continue down the side of your work (1 sc in the side of each row): [sc 2, ch 6, starting in 2nd ch from hook: slst 5] 12x, sc 1, ch 4, starting in 2nd ch from hook: slst 3, sc 3 (the 2nd sc will be the tr inc from Row 61), ch 4, starting in 2nd ch from hook: slst 3, sc 1, [ch 6, starting in 2nd ch from hook: slst 5, sc 2] 13x, tr inc into the tr dec at the tip of the head piece, Continue down the back side of the head piece: sc 24, continue down the body: sc 50, tr inc in tip, continue up the side of the body: sc 50, continue up the back side of the head piece: sc 24, slst to the first stitch of this round.
Finishing Off	Cut and tie off, leaving very long tail for sewing.

Row 61	Working 1 sc in the side of each row: sc 8, ch 1 and turn (8 st)
Row 62	Sc 8, ch 1 and turn (8 st)
Row 63	Sc 7, inc, ch 1 and turn (9 st)
Row 64	Inc, sc 8, ch 1 and turn (10 st)
Row 65-66	Sc 10, ch 1 and turn (10 st per row) (2 rows)
Row 67	Inc, sc 7, dec, ch 1 and turn (10 st)
Row 68	Dec, sc 7, inc, ch 1 and turn (10 st)
Row 69	Inc, sc 7, dec, ch 1 and turn (10 st)
Row 70	Dec, sc 7, inc, ch 1 and turn (10 st)
Row 71	Sc 8, dec, ch 1 and turn (9 st)
Row 72	Dec, sc 6, inc, ch 1 and turn (9 st)
Row 73	Sc 7, dec, ch 1 and turn (8 st)
Row 74	Dec, sc 5, inc, ch 1 and turn (8 st)

END RESULT

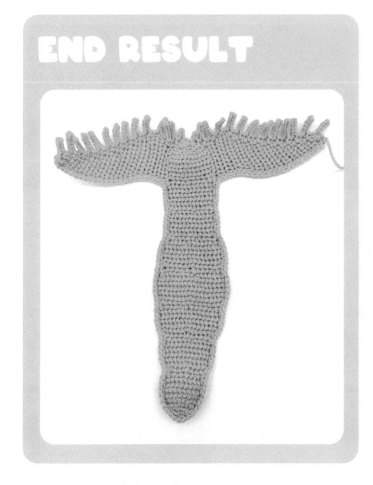

UNDERSIDE

Use **stomach color** yarn.

Row 1	Ch 2, sc 3 in 2nd ch from hook, ch 1 and turn (3 st)
Row 2	Inc 3, ch 1 and turn (6 st)
Row 3	[Sc 1, inc] 3x, ch 1 and turn (9 st)
Row 4-10	Sc 9, ch 1 and turn (9 st per row) (7 rows)
Row 11	Inc, sc 3, inc, sc 3, inc, ch 1 and turn (12 st)
Row 12-57	Sc 12 (12 st per row) (46 rows)
Row 58	[Sc 2, dec] 3x, ch 1 and turn (9 st)
Row 59	[Sc 1, dec] 3x, ch 1 and turn (6 st)
Row 60	Dec 3, ch 1 and turn (3 st)

Row 61	Trp dec, work down the side of your work (1 sc in the side of each row): sc 10, ch 1 and turn (11 st)
Row 62	Sc 8, ch 1 and turn (8 st)
Row 63	Inc, sc 7, ch 1 and turn (9 st)
Row 64	Sc 8, inc, ch 1 and turn (10 st)
Row 65-66	Sc 10, ch 1 and turn (10 st per row) (2 rows)
Row 67	Dec, sc 7, inc, ch 1 and turn (10 st)
Row 68	Inc, sc 7, dec, ch 1 and turn (10 st)
Row 69	Dec, sc 7, inc, ch 1 and turn (10 st)
Row 70	Inc, sc 7, dec, ch 1 and turn (10 st)
Row 71	Dec, sc 8, ch 1 and turn (9 st)
Row 72	Inc, sc 6, dec, ch 1 and turn (9 st)
Row 73	Dec, sc 7, ch 1 and turn (8 st)
Row 74	Inc, sc 5, dec, ch 1 and turn (8 st)
Row 75	Dec, sc 6, ch 1 and turn (7 st)
Row 76	Inc, sc 4, dec, ch 1 and turn (7 st)
Row 77	Dec, sc 5, ch 1 and turn (6 st)
Row 78	Inc, sc 3, dec, ch 1 and turn (6 st)
Row 79	Dec, sc 4, ch 1 and turn (5 st)
Row 80	Inc, sc 2, dec, ch 1 and turn (5 st)
Row 81	Dec, sc 3, ch 1 and turn (4 st)
Row 82	Inc, sc, dec, ch 1 and turn (4 st)
Row 83	Dec, sc 2, ch 1 and turn (3 st)

Row 84	Inc, dec, ch 1 and turn (3 st)
Row 85	Trp dec (1 st)
Finishing Off	Cut and tie off, weave in end.

END RESULT

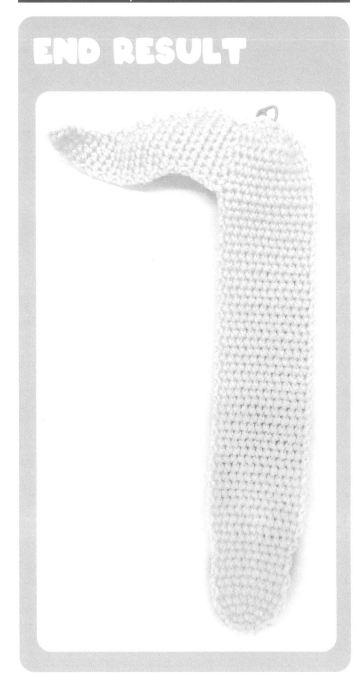

Reattaching Yarn for 2nd Head Piece	Take note of the row where your last sc of Row 61 was (this should be around the 10th row back from the tr dec of Row 61), and reattach your yarn to the side of this row. You will make your first stitch in this stitch. The rows will continue numbering at 61 so that the numbers of this piece match the numbers of the first head piece for easy reference and comparison.

Row 61	Working 1 sc in the side of each row: sc 8, ch 1 and turn (8 st)
Row 62	Sc 8, ch 1 and turn (8 st)
Row 63	Sc 7, inc, ch 1 and turn (9 st)
Row 64	Inc, sc 8, ch 1 and turn (10 st)
Row 65-66	Sc 10, ch 1 and turn (10 st per row) (2 rows)

Row 67	Inc, sc 7, dec, ch 1 and turn (10 st)
Row 68	Dec, sc 7, inc, ch 1 and turn (10 st)
Row 69	Inc, sc 7, dec, ch 1 and turn (10 st)
Row 70	Dec, sc 7, inc, ch 1 and turn (10 st)
Row 71	Sc 8, dec, ch 1 and turn (9 st)
Row 72	Dec, sc 6, inc, ch 1 and turn (9 st)
Row 73	Sc 7, dec, ch 1 and turn (8 st)
Row 74	Dec, sc 5, inc, ch 1 and turn (8 st)
Row 75	Sc 6, dec, ch 1 and turn (7 st)
Row 76	Dec, sc 4, inc, ch 1 and turn (7 st)
Row 77	Sc 5, dec, ch 1 and turn (6 st)
Row 78	Dec, sc 3, inc, ch 1 and turn (6 st)
Row 79	Sc 4, dec, ch 1 and turn (5 st)
Row 80	Dec, sc 2, inc, ch 1 and turn (5 st)
Row 81	Sc 3, dec, ch 1 and turn (4 st)
Row 82	Dec, sc 1, inc, ch 1 and turn (4 st)
Row 83	Sc 2, dec, ch 1 and turn (3 st)
Row 84	Dec, inc, ch 1 and turn (3 st)

*Round 85 (Border Round)	Tr dec, continue down the side of your work (1 sc in the side of each row): sc 53 (the 27th stitch will be the tr dec from Row 1), tr inc in the tip of the head piece, continue down the back of the head piece: sc 24, continue down the body: sc 50, tr inc, continue up the side of the body: sc 50, continue up the back side of the head piece: sc 24, slst to the first stitch of this round.
Finishing Off	Cut and tie off, weave in ends.

END RESULT

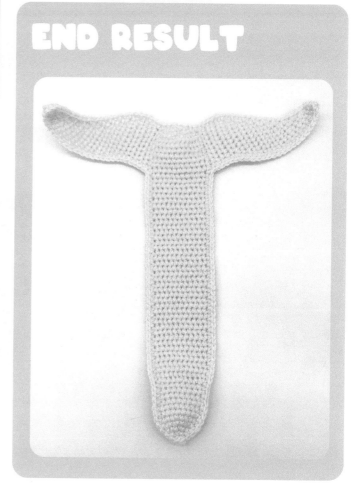

117

FLIPPER PIECES (MAKE 2)

Use **back color** yarn. You will be making 6 flippers for each side of the body. Make 5 flippers and set them aside. Then in the 6th flipper, keep your hook active in the piece. You will then crochet together all 6 pieces in a line.

END RESULT

Flippers 1-5	Make 5
Row 1	Ch 2, sc 1 in 2nd ch from hook, ch 1 and turn (1 st)
Row 2	Inc, ch 1 and turn (2 st)
Row 3	2/3 inc, ch 1 and turn (3 st)
Row 4	Sc 1, inc, sc, ch 1 and turn (4 st)
Row 5	Sc 1, 2/3 inc, sc 1, ch 1 and turn (5 st)
Row 6	Sc 2, inc, sc 2, ch 1 and turn (6 st)
Row 7-8	Sc 6, ch 1 and turn (6 st per row) (2 rows)
*Round 9 (Border Round)	Sc 5, tr inc, continue down the side of your work: sc 7, tr inc in tip, continue up side: sc 7, inc, slst to first stitch of this round (27 st)
Finishing Off	Cut and tie off, weave in ends.

Flipper 6	
Row 1	Ch 2, sc 1 in 2nd ch from hook, ch 1 and turn (1 st)
Row 2	Inc, ch 1 and turn (2 st)
Row 3	2/3 inc, ch 1 and turn (3 st)
Row 4	Sc 1, inc, sc, ch 1 and turn (4 st)
Row 5	Sc 1, 2/3 inc, sc 1, ch 1 and turn (5 st)
Row 6	Sc 2, inc, sc 2, ch 1 and turn (6 st)
Row 7-8	Sc 6, ch 1 and turn (6 st per row) (2 rows)
*Round 9 (Border Round)	Sc 5, tr inc, continue down the side of your work: sc 7, tr inc in tip, continue up side: sc 7, inc, slst to first stitch of this round (27 st)

*Row 10 (Connecting Row)	Ch 1, starting in the first stitch of Round 9: sc 5, dec, [start in the first available stitch of another flipper (The first stitch of the Border Round of the flipper): sc 5, dec] 5x, ch 1 and turn (36 st)
Row 11	Sc 35, dec (36 st)
Finishing Off	Cut and tie off, weave in ends.

END RESULT

ASSEMBLING BODY

Stem Wire	Cut a length of stem wire that circles the entire border of the body part of the yellow piece (exclude the head pieces) and tape it into a closed ring, as shown in the photo below. For added security, use a piece of **stomach color** yarn to sew it down in a few spots to ensure that it does not move around in the finished piece.

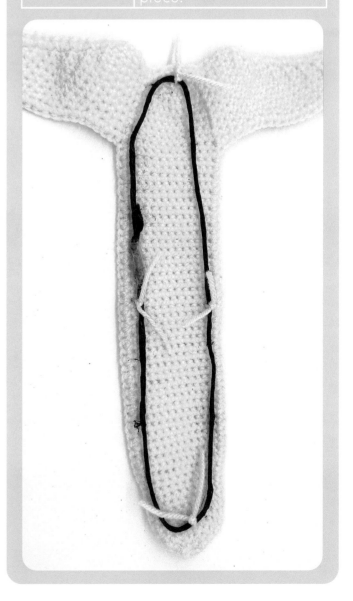

119

Alignment of Flipper Pieces	Place the flipper pieces along the border of the underside piece. The backmost stitch of the flipper will connect to the third stitch away from the very center stitch of the underside (the back end of the body). Pin it in place using stitch markers.

| Placement & Sewing of Back | Place the back piece over the top of the underside so that it aligns with the underside piece. (Fig 1 on pg. 121)

Then, use your long yarn tail from the Back piece to begin sewing the two pieces together using seamless sewing technique. Start by going around the front of the head and get that sewn together before you head towards the part where the flippers are attached. This will give you a solid foundation sewn together that will make it easier to align the flipper pieces. Work around the bristle pieces on the front of the head and just work into the sc stitches in between.

Sew until you get to the corner where the head piece ends and the body begins. (Fig. 2 on pg. 121) Stuff the left head piece. Then, sew as before in the next 12 stitches, then stop. This is where the flipper part begins. |
| --- | --- |

FIG. 1

FIG. 2

FIG. 3

| Placement & Sewing of Back Cont. | To sew the flipper part into the whole seam, you are going to continue sewing using the <u>seamless sewing technique</u>, but you are going to go through the stitches of the Row 11 part of the flipper piece as you do it. Make sure that when you go from both Back to Underside, and Underside to back, you are passing through the next available stitch of the flipper piece's Row 11 to make this seam nice and strong. Be sure to pull nice and tight to avoid gaps. You will sew through 36 stitches in this manner. (See Fig. 3 on pg. 121)

Once you reach the end of the first flipper piece, you will return to working only through the Back and Underside pieces for 7 stitches. Then, you will start working through the first stitch of the second flipper piece the same way you did with the first one. Stuff the body as you go.

Once you reach the end of the second flipper piece, finish sewing the rest of the perimeter shut the same way you sewed the rest of the non-flipper edges shut. Give the flippers a nice stretch to flatten them out. |
|---|---|

END RESULT

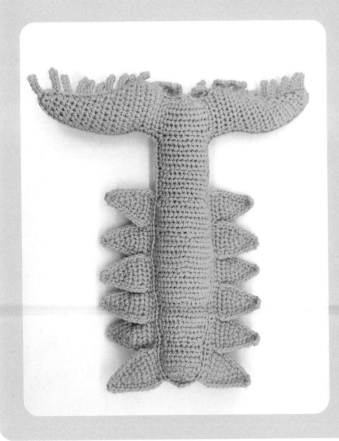
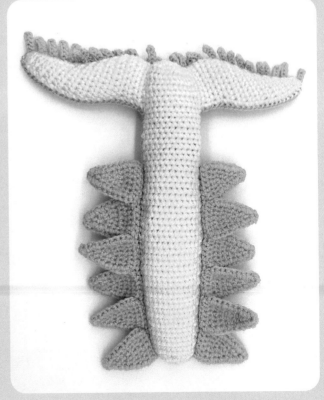

LEG PIECES (MAKE 2)

Use **stomach color** yarn. You will make 6 legs on each side for a total of 12 legs. You will then crochet them together in a line. This will make sewing them on much less tedious!

Make first five legs and then set them aside. You will keep your hook active in the final leg so that you can crochet them all together.

Legs 1-5	Make 5
Round 1	Ch 2, sc 6 in 2nd ch from hook (6 st)
Round 2	BLO: Sc 6 (6 st)
Round 3	BLO: [Sc 1, inc] 3x (9 st)
Round 4	BLO: Sc 9 (9 st)
Round 5	BLO: [Sc 2, inc] 3x (12 st)
Round 6-8	BLO: Sc 12 (12 st per round) (3 rounds)
Finishing Off	Cut and tie off, weave in end.

Leg 6	
Round 1	Ch 2, sc 6 in 2nd ch from hook (6 st)
Round 2	BLO: Sc 6 (6 st)
Round 3	BLO: [Sc 1, inc] 3x (9 st)
Round 4	BLO: Sc 9 (9 st)
Round 5	BLO: [Sc 2, inc] 3x (12 st)
Round 6-8	BLO: Sc 12 (12 st per round) (3 rounds)
Round 9 (Joining Round)	Sc 6, ch 2, [starting in the first available stitch of one of your other legs: sc 6, ch 2] 4x, starting in the first available stitch of your last leg: sc 12, [work into the back of the chains: sc 2, starting in the first available stitch of the next leg: sc 6] 5x
Finishing Off	Slst to next st, cut and tie off, leaving long tail for sewing. Lightly stuff all of the legs.

END RESULT

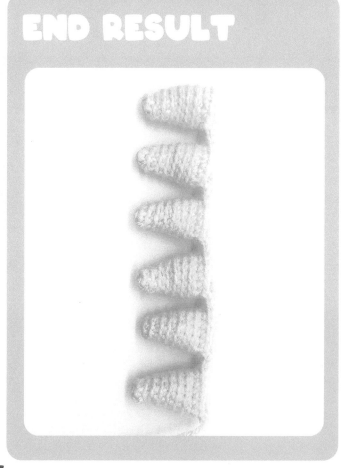

ATTACHING LEG PIECES TO UNDERSIDE

Alignment	Flip the body over so that the yellow underside is facing up. Then, place the leg pieces onto each side of the body with the backmost leg about 4 rows forward from the very tip of the back of the body. There should be about 5 stitches of space between the leg pieces.
Sewing	Use whip stitch sewing technique.

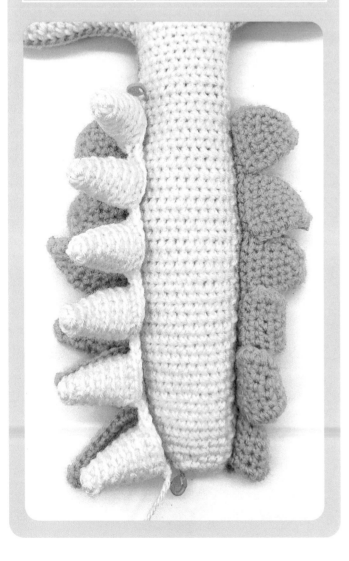

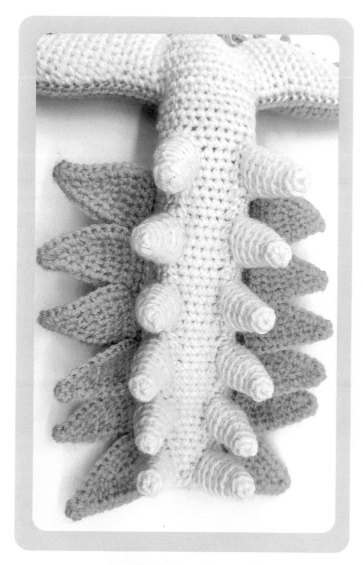

Round 1	Ch 2, sc 24 in the 2nd ch from hook (24 st)
Finishing Off	Slst to next st, cut and tie off, leaving long tail for sewing, weave in the other end.

END RESULT

MOUTH PIECE

Use **stomach color** yarn.

Technique Explanation	You are going to be working far too many stitches than would normally fit into the round to achieve a specific look. Once you hit 6 sc in the round, you will continue making sc stitches in the starting chain space that enclose the stitches made before it. As you go, you will have to make your stitches bigger and bigger to encase the stitches you have made inside this chain space. The result will be a thick doughnut shape.

ATTACHING MOUTH PIECE TO FACE

Alignment	Center the mouth piece on the front of the head just a few rows down from the edge where the Back and Underside pieces join. The wrong side of the round will be facing outward, while the right side will be against the surface of the head.
Sewing	Use whip stitch sewing technique.

EMBROIDERING SPOTS (OPTIONAL)

Embroidery	Cut a long piece of accent color yarn. Embroider spots at random parts all over the back of the Pambdelurion by wrapping your yarn around 1-2 stitches of the back about 3-4 times to make a rounded spot.

126

FINAL PRODUCT

Your Pambdelurion is officially complete! Check out the gallery below to make sure your piece came out as intended.

GALLERY

MARRELLA

(Muh-RELL-uh)

MATERIALS

2.5 mm Crochet Hook (or hook size of your choice)
Yarn (All Worsted Weight):

Head Color	Less than 1/2 of a 364 yd skein
Body Color	Less than 1/2 of a 364 yd skein
Feather Color	Less than 1/4 of a 364 yd skein

Stuffing
Stem Wire
Darning Needle
Stitch Marker
Sewing Pins

WHAT WAS MARRELLA?

Marrella was a highly unusual arthropod creature. It was so unlike anything else alive at the time that its group is called "Marrellomorph". It is the most common creature found in the Burgess Shale, with tens of thousands of fossils being found there. It even has its own layer dedicated to it, known as the "Marrella Bed", or "Marrella Layer".

When it was first discovered, paleontologists were not quite sure how to classify it. Marrella discoverer Charles Doolittle Walcott called it a "lace crab" and believed it to be an unusual trilobite form, but upon further study of its body parts, it was determined that it was nowhere near a trilobite or a crustacean of any kind.

Marrellas were very tiny, ranging from 1/10th of an inch to just shy of an inch (2.54 cm) long. The body had anywhere from 17-28 segments depending on the specimen.

They were active swimmers that stayed close to the seafloor, a behavior referred to as "nektobenthic". They were most likely filter feeders and would likely have been preyed upon by larger creatures. It used its front appendages to swim around and its head spines probably helped to stabilize it in the water.

Some well-preserved specimens of Marrella show evidence that it may have had an iridescent color, but this theory has not been confirmed and is debated by other scientists. Some other specimens have been found in the process of molting, which indicates that they would shed their outer layers like modern-day insects, reptiles, and crustaceans.

Finished Size:
Approx. 12 in
(30 cm) long
and 5 inches
(13 cm) tall,
Results may vary
depending on
individual tension.

DIFFICULTY:

ADVANCED

HEAD PIECE

Use **head color** yarn. Stuff the piece as you go. Check out the invisible join tutorial listed on the terminology page!

Round 1	Ch 6, starting in 2nd ch from hook: tr inc, sc 3, tr inc, continue along the bottom of the stitches you just made starting with the one you just worked your last tr inc into: tr inc, sc 3, tr inc, invisible join, ch 1 (18 st)
Important Technique Note	Working in FLO and BLO are absolutely essential to keeping your shape square, but in addition to this, ending each round with [slst to beg st, ch 1] is also crucial. In many patterns it is just a matter of preference, but in this one, it can make or break your alignment if you do not abide by it.
Round 2	FLO: [sc 1, tr inc, sc 1], sc 3, [sc, tr inc, sc] 2x, sc 3, [sc, tr inc, sc], invisible join, ch 1 (26 st)
Round 3	FLO: [Sc 2, tr inc, sc 2], sc 3, [sc 2, tr inc, sc 2] 2x, sc 3 [sc 2, tr inc, sc 2], invisible join, ch 1 (34 st)
Round 4	BLO: Sc 34, invisible join, ch 1 (34 st)
Round 5-14	FLO: Sc 34, invisible join, ch 1 (34 st per round) (10 rounds)
Round 15	FLO: Sc 34, DO NOT SLST TO BEG ST AND CH 1 (34 st) *You will begin working in spiral rounds in Round 16 (i.e. no more slst to beg st, ch 1)*
*Row 16	FLO: Sc 5, turn without chaining (5 st)
Row 17-23	Skip first stitch, sc 9, turn without chaining (9 st per row) (7 rows) *For the last stitch of rows 18-23, you will be dropping down into the next available stitch from Round 15*
*Round 24	Sc 26 (26 st)
Round 25	FLO: Starting in the first st of Round 24: sc 12, inc 3, sc 4, inc 3, sc 4 (32 st)
Round 26-27	FLO: Sc 32 (32 st per round) (2 rounds)
Round 28	FLO: Sc 5, skip 16 st, sc 11 (16 st) *You will be closing off into a smaller round*
Round 29	FLO: Sc 1, dec 3, sc 4, inc 3, sc 2 (16 st)
Round 30	FLO: Sc 16 (16 st)
Round 31	FLO: Dec 3, sc 3, inc 3, sc 4 (16 st)
Round 32	FLO: Sc 16 (16 st)
Round 33	FLO: Dec 2, sc 4, inc 3, sc 3, dec (16 st)
Round 34-43	Sc 16 (16 st per round) (10 rounds)
Round 44	[Sc 2, dec] 4x (12 st)
Round 45-54	Sc 12 (12 st per round) (10 rounds)
Round 55	[Sc 2, dec] 3x (9 st)
Round 56-60	Sc 9 (9 st per round) (5 rounds)
Round 61	[Sc 1, dec] 3x (6 st)
Round 62-66	Sc 6 (6 st per round) (5 rounds)
Round 67	[Sc 1, dec] 2x (4 st)
Round 68-69	Sc 4 (4 st per round) (2 rounds)
Finishing Off	Slst to next st, cut and tie off, sew the remaining hole of the point closed, weave in end

END RESULT

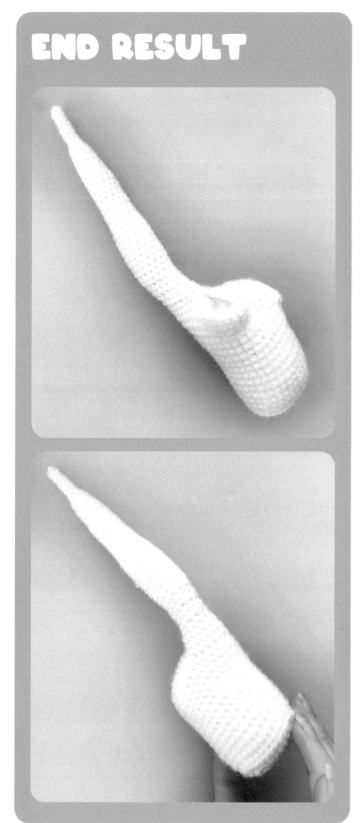

Round 28	FLO: Sc 16 (16 st)
Round 29	FLO: Dec, sc 4, inc 3, sc 3, dec 2 (16 st)
Round 30	FLO: Sc 16 (16 st)
Round 31	FLO: Dec 2, sc 4, inc 3, sc 3, dec (16 st)
Round 32	FLO: Sc 16 (16 st)
Round 33	FLO: Dec 3, sc 3, inc 3, sc 4 (16 st)
Round 34-43	Sc 16 (16 st per round) (10 rounds)
Round 44	[Sc 2, dec] 4x (12 st)
Round 45-54	Sc 12 (12 st per round) (10 rounds)

Round 55	[Sc 2, dec] 3x (9 st)
Round 56-60	Sc 9 (9 st per round) (5 rounds)
Round 61	[Sc 1, dec] 3x (6 st)
Round 62-66	Sc 6 (6 st per round) (5 rounds)
Round 67	[Sc 1, dec] 2x (4 st)
Round 68-69	Sc 4 (4 st per round) (2 rounds)
Finishing Off	Slst to next st, cut and tie off, sew the remaining hole of the point closed, weave in end

END RESULT

SIDE TENTACLES (MAKE 2)

Use **head color** yarn. Stuff the piece as you go.

Round 1	Ch 2, sc 4 in 2nd ch from hook (4 st)
Round 2-3	Sc 4 (4 st per round) (2 rounds)
Round 4	[Sc 1, inc] 2x (6 st)
Round 5-9	Sc 6 (6 st per round) (5 rounds)
Round 10	[Sc 1, inc] 3x (9 st)
Round 11-15	Sc 9 (9 st per round) (5 rounds)
Round 16	[Sc 2, inc] 3x (12 st)
Round 17-21	Sc 12 (12 st per round) (5 rounds)
Technique Note	From this point on onward, work all of your sc stitches in the Front Loops Only. This will keep the curve we are about to create from twisting and warping over time.
Round 22	Slst 4, sc 8 (12 st)
Round 23	Ddsc 4, sc 8 (12 st)
Round 24	Sc 12 (12 st)
Round 25	Slst 4, sc 8 (12 st)
Round 26	Ddsc 4, sc 8 (12 st)
Round 27	Sc 12 (12 st)
Round 28	Slst 4, sc 8 (12 st)
Round 29	Ddsc 4, sc 8 (12 st)
Round 30	[Sc 3, inc] 3x (15 st)
Round 31	Slst 5, sc 10 (15 st)
Round 32	Ddsc 5, sc 10 (15 st)
Round 33	[Sc 4, inc] 3x (18 st)
Round 34	Slst 6, sc 12 (18 st)
Round 35	Ddsc 6, sc 12 (18 st)
Round 36-37	Sc 18 (18 st per round) (2 rounds)
Finishing Off	Slst to next st, cut and tie off, leaving long tail for sewing

END RESULT

ATTACHING SIDE TENTACLES TO HEAD PIECE

Alignment	Place the opening of the side tentacles onto the side of the front of the head piece with the point of the tentacle facing backwards. The front edge should be flush with Round 6 of the head.
Sewing	Use <u>whip stitch sewing technique</u>.

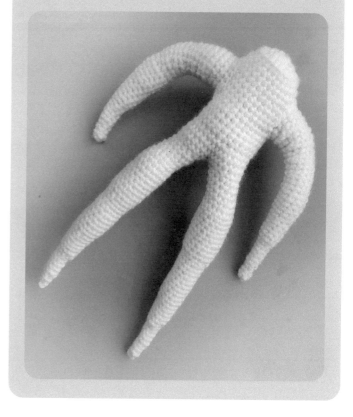

BODY

Use **body color** yarn. Stuff the piece as you go.

Round 42	Inc 12 (24 st)
Round 43	[Sc 3, inc] 6x (30 st)
Round 44-48	Sc 30 (30 st per round) (5 rounds)
Round 49	Dec 15 (15 st)
Finishing Off	Slst to next st, cut and tie off, leaving long tail for sewing

Technique Note	Work ALL stitches in Front Loops Only. This will keep all of your stitches perfectly straight and square, which will make the surface crochet that comes later much easier to keep straight. Your feather pieces will be super crooked or twisted if you do not follow this step!
Round 1	Ch 2, sc 6 in 2nd ch from hook (6 st)
Round 2	Sc 6 (6 st)
Round 3	[Sc 1, inc] 3x (9 st)
Round 4	Sc 9 (9 st)
Round 5	[Sc 2, inc] 3x (12 st)
Round 6-8	Sc 12 (12 st per round) (3 rounds)
Round 9	Dec 6 (6 st)
Round 10	Inc 6 (12 st)
Round 11-16	Sc 12 (12 st per round) (6 rounds)
Round 17	Dec 6 (6 st)
Round 18	Inc 6 (12 st)
Round 19	[Sc 1, inc] 6x (18 st)
Round 20-24	Sc 18 (18 st per round) (5 rounds)
Round 25	Dec 9 (9 st)
Round 26	Inc 9 (18 st)
Round 27-32	Sc 18 (18 st per round) (6 rounds)
Round 33	Dec 9 (9 st)
Round 34	Inc 9 (18 st)
Round 35	[Sc 2, inc] 6x (24 st)
Round 36-40	Sc 24 (24 st per round) (5 rounds)
Round 41	Dec 12 (12 st)

END RESULT

CREATING FEATHER PIECES ON BODY (SIDE 1)

Start with **head color** yarn. You will switch to **feather color** yarn when prompted and then work with both colors using <u>tapestry crochet color changing technique</u>. **Feather Color** stitches will be notated by an F and **Head Color** stitches will be notated by an H. You will be surface crocheting down the side of the body for the first row.

Attaching Yarn	Attach your yarn to any of the available stitches from Round 49 of the body and chain 1. You will be working around the posts of the stitches as you go down, working 1 sc in the side of each round.
Row 1	Sc 45, ch 5 and turn (45 st) *You will be stopping a few rounds short from the tip. Also, when you see **return to surface** in Row 2, this will mean to continue working into the next available stitch of the surface crocheted stitches from Row 1*
Row 2	Starting in the 2nd ch from hook: sc 4, return to surface: sc 4, ch 5, starting in 2nd ch from hook: sc 4, return to surface: sc 4, [Ch 6, starting in 2nd ch from hook: sc 5, return to surface: sc 4] 2x, [Ch 7, starting in 2nd ch from hook: sc 6, return to surface: sc 4] 2x, [Ch 8, starting in 2nd ch from hook: sc 7, return to surface: sc 4] 2x, ...
Row 2 cont.	[Ch 9, starting in 2nd ch from hook: sc 8, return to surface: sc 4] 2x, Ch 10, starting in 2nd ch from hook: sc 9, return to surface: sc 4, ch 10, starting in 2nd ch from hook: sc 9, return to surface: sc 1 *Switch to **feather color** yarn, CH 1 AND TURN* (You should have 12 feather stems)

END RESULT

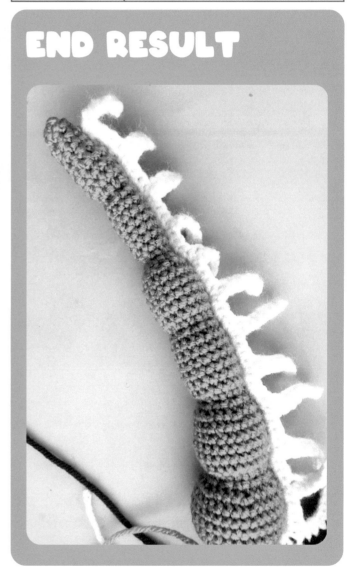

135

Row 3	Carry the **head color** yarn in the single crochet stitches as you begin working, don't carry it in the slip stitches. **Feather 1**: [F: Ch 4, starting in 2nd ch from hook: slst 3, return to row: sc 1] 9x, ch 4, starting in 2nd ch from hook: slst 3, sc in the same stitch as your last sc stitch, continue along the other side of the white feather stem (working your sc stitches in the bottom of the stitches of the white feather stem), [F: Ch 4, starting in 2nd ch from hook: slst 3, return to row: sc 1] 9x, H: sc 4 **Feather 2**: *Repeat Feather 1 again on the second white feather stem* **Feather 3**: [F: Ch 4, starting in 2nd ch from hook: slst 3, return to row: sc 1] 8x, ch 4, starting in 2nd ch from hook: slst 3, sc in the same stitch as your last sc stitch, continue along the other side of the white feather stem (working your sc stitches in the bottom of the stitches of the white feather stem), [F: Ch 4, starting in 2nd ch from hook: slst 3, return to row: sc 1] 8x, H: sc 4 **Feather 4**: *Repeat Feather 3 again on the fourth white feather stem* ...

Row 3 cont.	**Feather 5**: [F: Ch 4, starting in 2nd ch from hook: slst 3, return to row: sc 1] 7x, ch 4, starting in 2nd ch from hook: slst 3, sc in the same stitch as your last sc stitch, continue along the other side of the white feather stem (working your sc stitches in the bottom of the stitches of the white feather stem), [F: Ch 4, starting in 2nd ch from hook: slst 3, return to row: sc 1] 7x, H: sc 4 **Feather 6**: *Repeat Feather 5 again on the sixth white feather stem* **Feather 7**: [F: Ch 4, starting in 2nd ch from hook: slst 3, return to row: sc 1] 6x, ch 4, starting in 2nd ch from hook: slst 3, sc in the same stitch as your last sc stitch, continue along the other side of the white feather stem (working your sc stitches in the bottom of the stitches of the white feather stem), [F: Ch 4, starting in 2nd ch from hook: slst 3, return to row: sc 1] 6x, H: sc 4 **Feather 8**: *Repeat Feather 7 again on the eight white feather stem* ...

Row 3 cont.	**Feather 9**: [F: Ch 4, starting in 2nd ch from hook: slst 3, return to row: sc 1] 5x, ch 4, starting in 2nd ch from hook: slst 3, sc in the same stitch as your last sc stitch, continue along the other side of the white feather stem (working your sc stitches in the bottom of the stitches of the white feather stem), [F: Ch 4, starting in 2nd ch from hook: slst 3, return to row: sc 1] 5x, H: sc 4 **Feather 10**: *Repeat Feather 9 again on the tenth white feather stem* **Feather 11**: [F: Ch 4, starting in 2nd ch from hook: slst 3, return to row: sc 1] 4x, ch 4, starting in 2nd ch from hook: slst 3, sc in the same stitch as your last sc stitch, continue along the other side of the white feather stem (working your sc stitches in the bottom of the stitches of the white feather stem), [F: Ch 4, starting in 2nd ch from hook: slst 3, return to row: sc 1] 4x, H: sc 4 **Feather 12**: [F: Ch 4, starting in 2nd ch from hook: slst 3, return to row: sc 1] 4x, ch 4, starting in 2nd ch from hook: slst 3, sc in the same stitch as your last sc stitch, continue along the other side of the white feather stem (working your sc stitches in the bottom of the stitches of the white feather stem), [F: Ch 4, starting in 2nd ch from hook: slst 3, return to row: sc 1] 4x

Finishing Off	Cut and tie off, leaving long tail for sewing, weave in the **head color** end.

END RESULT

Sewing Feathers Flat	Flatten out all of the feathers and overlap them on each other with the longest feather on top and the shortest one on the bottom. Then, use the long sewing tail and zig zag along, going through a few stitches of each of the feathers towards their ends to secure them in this flattened overlapping state.

END RESULT

CREATING FEATHER PIECES ON BODY (SIDE 2)

Start with **head color** yarn. You will switch to **feather color** yarn when prompted and then work with both colors using tapestry crochet color changing technique. **Feather Color** stitches will be notated by an F and **Head Color** stitches will be notated by an H. You will be surface crocheting down the side of the body for the first row.

Attaching Yarn	YOU WILL BE ATTACHING AT A DIFFERENT POINT THAN THE FIRST SIDE. Take note of where the first feather side ends towards the tip of the body piece. Reattach your yarn on the opposite side of the stitch where the first feather side ends, which should be around Round 3 of the body piece. You will surface crochet up the side towards the open end of the body.
Row 1	Sc 45, ch 10 and turn (45 st) *You will be stopping right at the open edge of the body. Also, when you see **return to surface** in Row 2, this will mean to continue working into the next available stitch of the surface crocheted stitches from Row 1*
Row 2	Starting in the 2nd ch from hook: sc 9, return to surface: sc 4, ch 10, starting in 2nd ch from hook: sc 9, return to surface: sc 4, [Ch 9, starting in 2nd ch from hook: sc 8, return to surface: sc 4] 2x, [Ch 8, starting in 2nd ch from hook: sc 7, return to surface: sc 4] 2x, [Ch 7, starting in 2nd ch from hook: sc 6, return to surface: sc 4] 2x, [Ch 6, starting in 2nd ch from hook: sc 5, return to surface: sc 4] 2x, ...

Row 2 cont.	Ch 5, starting in 2nd ch from hook: sc 4, return to surface: sc 4, ch 5, starting in 2nd ch from hook: sc 4, return to surface: sc 1 *Switch to **feather color** yarn, CH 1 AND TURN* (You should have 12 feather stems)
Row 3	Carry the head color yarn in the single crochet stitches as you begin working, don't carry it in the slip stitches. **Feather 1**: [F: Ch 4, starting in 2nd ch from hook: slst 3, return to row: sc 1] 4x, ch 4, starting in 2nd ch from hook: slst 3, sc in the same stitch as your last sc stitch, continue along the other side of the white feather stem (working your sc stitches in the bottom of the stitches of the white feather stem), [F: Ch 4, starting in 2nd ch from hook: slst 3, return to row: sc 1] 4x, H: sc 4 **Feather 2**: *Repeat Feather 1 again on the second white feather stem **Feather 3**: [F: Ch 4, starting in 2nd ch from hook: slst 3, return to row: sc 1] 5x, ch 4, starting in 2nd ch from hook: slst 3, sc in the same stitch as your last sc stitch, continue along the other side of the white feather stem (working your sc stitches in the bottom of the stitches of the white feather stem), [F: Ch 4, starting in 2nd ch from hook: slst 3, return to row: sc 1] 5x, H: sc 4 ...
Row 3 cont.	**Feather 4**: *Repeat Feather 3 again on the fourth white feather stem* **Feather 5**: [F: Ch 4, starting in 2nd ch from hook: slst 3, return to row: sc 1] 6x, ch 4, starting in 2nd ch from hook: slst 3, sc in the same stitch as your last sc stitch, continue along the other side of the white feather stem (working your sc stitches in the bottom of the stitches of the white feather stem), [F: Ch 4, starting in 2nd ch from hook: slst 3, return to row: sc 1] 6x, H: sc 4 **Feather 6**: *Repeat Feather 5 on the sixth white feather stem* **Feather 7**: [F: Ch 4, starting in 2nd ch from hook: slst 3, return to row: sc 1] 7x, ch 4, starting in 2nd ch from hook: slst 3, sc in the same stitch as your last sc stitch, continue along the other side of the white feather stem (working your sc stitches in the bottom of the stitches of the white feather stem), [F: Ch 4, starting in 2nd ch from hook: slst 3, return to row: sc 1] 7x, H: sc 4 **Feather 8**: *Repeat Feather 7 on the eighth white feather stem* ...

Row 3 cont.	**Feather 9**: [F: Ch 4, starting in 2nd ch from hook: slst 3, return to row: sc 1] 8x, ch 4, starting in 2nd ch from hook: slst 3, sc in the same stitch as your last sc stitch, continue along the other side of the white feather stem (working your sc stitches in the bottom of the stitches of the white feather stem), [F: Ch 4, starting in 2nd ch from hook: slst 3, return to row: sc 1] 8x, H: sc 4 **Feather 10**: *Repeat Feather 9 on the tenth white feather stem* **Feather 11**: [F: Ch 4, starting in 2nd ch from hook: slst 3, return to row: sc 1] 9x, ch 4, starting in 2nd ch from hook: slst 3, sc in the same stitch as your last sc stitch, continue along the other side of the white feather stem (working your sc stitches in the bottom of the stitches of the white feather stem), [F: Ch 4, starting in 2nd ch from hook: slst 3, return to row: sc 1] 9x, H: sc 4 **Feather 12**: [F: Ch 4, starting in 2nd ch from hook: slst 3, return to row: sc 1] 9x, ch 4, starting in 2nd ch from hook: slst 3, sc in the same stitch as your last sc stitch, continue along the other side of the white feather stem (working your sc stitches in the bottom of the stitches of the white feather stem), [F: Ch 4, starting in 2nd ch from hook: slst 3, return to row: sc 1] 9x

Finishing Off	Cut and tie off, leaving long tail for sewing, weave in **head color** end.
Sewing Feathers Flat	Flatten out all of the feathers and overlap them on each other with the longest feather on top and the shortest one on the bottom. Then, use the long sewing tail and zig zag along, going through a few stitches of each of the feathers towards their ends to secure them in this flattened overlapping state.

END RESULT

LEG PIECES (MAKE 2)

Use **body color** yarn. You will be making 20 total individual legs and working together 10 each so that all of the legs on one side of the body will be one singular piece that can be sewn on as one. This will make the sewing process much less tedious! Do not stuff.

Legs 1-9	Make 9
Round 1	Ch 2, sc 6 in 2nd ch from hook (6 st)
Round 2-21	Sc 6 (6 st per round) (20 rounds)
Finishing Off	Cut and tie off, weave in end

Legs 10	
Round 1	Ch 2, sc 6 in 2nd ch from hook (6 st)
Round 2-21	Sc 6 (6 st per round) (20 rounds)
Round 22 (Joining Round)	[Ch 2, start in the first available stitch of one of your other legs: sc 3] 8x, ch 2, start in the first available stitch of the last available leg: sc 6, [work into the back of the chains: sc 2, start in the first available stitch of the next leg: sc 3] 9x (75 st)
Finishing Off	Cut and tie off, leaving long tail for sewing.

END RESULT

END RESULT

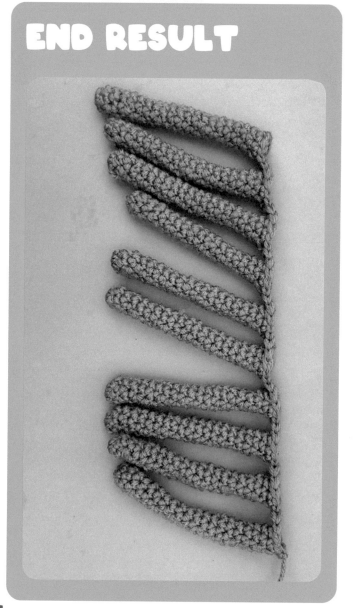

141

| Adding Stem Wire | Place a length of stem wire into each leg and trim it so that about half an inch sticks out of the opening of each leg. To make sure that the wire doesn't poke through the bottom of the legs, you can fold it over itself to make a more rounded end. Then, tightly wrap the exposed tip with scotch tape. You will be pushing the stem wire into the stitches of the body to make the joint stronger. Towards the back of the body you may need to trim your exposed ends shorter since the body is not as thick there. |

END RESULT

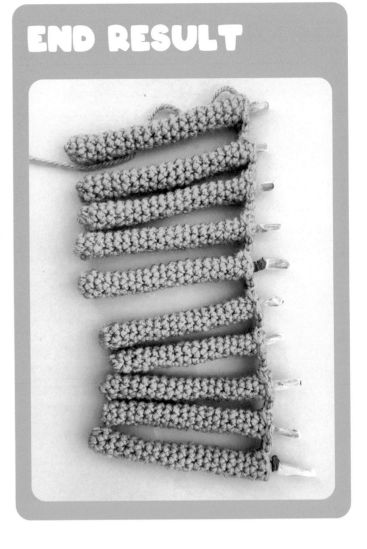

ATTACHING LEG PIECES TO BODY

Alignment	Place each leg piece on the bottom side of the body towards the base of where the feather parts attach to the body. Then, push the exposed stem wire tips of the first and last legs into the stitches of the body. This will give you an idea of where the rest of the legs in the middle should insert into the body. You may need to do some finagling to get them all in.
Sewing	Use whip stitch sewing technique around the entire Joining Round of the leg pieces to attach them to the body.

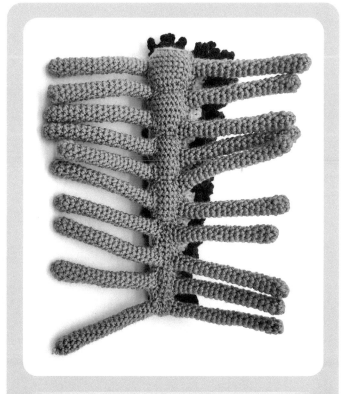

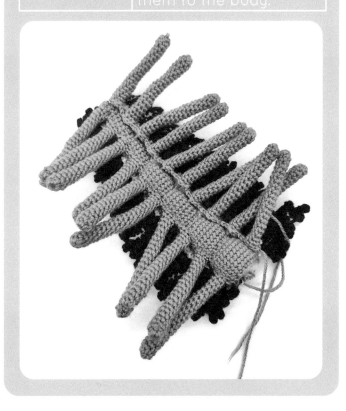

ATTACHING HEAD PIECE TO BODY

Alignment	Place the open hole of the body against the flat surface of the head piece that sits just below the middle two tentacles.

Sewing	Use seamless sewing technique.

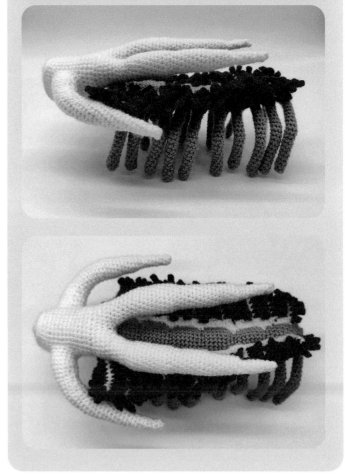

ANTENNAE (MAKE 2)

Use **body color** yarn. Do not stuff.

Round 1	Ch 2, sc 4 in 2nd ch from hook (4 st)
Round 2-11	BLO: Sc 4 (4 st per round) (10 rounds)
Round 12	BLO: [Sc 1, inc] 2x (6 st)
Round 13-32	BLO: Sc 6 (6 st per round) (20 rounds)
Finishing Off	Slst to next st, cut and tie off, leaving long tail for sewing. Insert a length of stem wire into the antenna and trim it so that about half an inch is still sticking out. Tightly wrap this end with Scotch tape to make insertion easier.

ATTACHING ANTENNAE TO HEAD PIECE

Alignment	Insert the stem wire of your antennae into the stitches of the head piece just below the Side Tentacle pieces.
Sewing	Use seamless sewing technique. After sewing it on, bend it so that it curves backwards like the side tentacles.

END RESULT

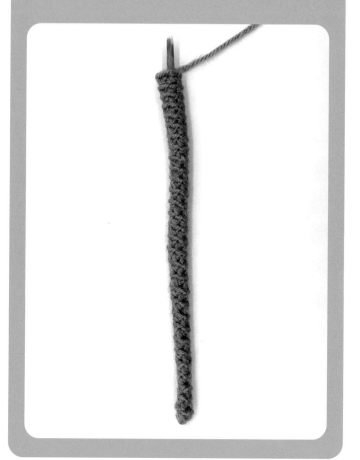

BRUSH APPENDAGES (MAKE 2)

Start with **body color** yarn. You will add on **head color** yarn when prompted to produce bristles.

Round 1	Ch 2, sc 6 in 2nd ch from hook (6 st)
Round 2-9	BLO: Sc 6 (6 st per round) (8 rounds)
Round 10-29	Sc 6 (6 st per round) (20 rounds)
Finishing Off	Slst to next st, cut and tie off, leaving long tail for sewing.
Reattaching With Head Color Yarn	Find the very last stitch that was worked into the back loops only before switching over to regular single crochet in Round 10. Attach your yarn to this loop. You will start the next round (Bristle Round) by chaining, working into those chains, and then single crocheting into the same loop that you attached your yarn to.
Bristle Round	Ch 4, starting in 2nd ch from hook: slst 3, sc into the same loop that you attached your yarn to, [ch 4, starting in 2nd ch from hook: slst 3, sc into the next available back loop] repeat this sequence in all of the back loops around the piece until you reach the tip.
Finishing Off	Cut and tie off, weave in **head color** end.

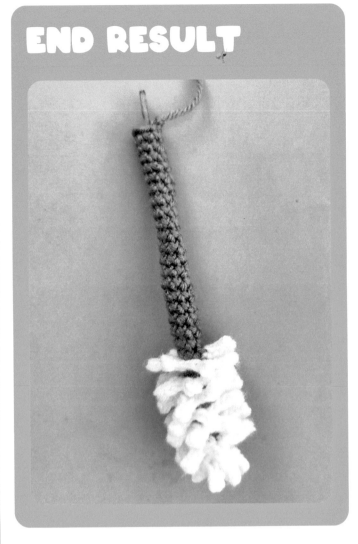

END RESULT

ATTACHING BRUSH APPENDAGES TO HEAD PIECE

Alignment	Insert the stem wire of the brush appendages into the head piece just behind the side tentacles.
Sewing	Use seamless sewing technique. After sewing it on, bend it so that it curves backwards like the side tentacles.

FINAL PRODUCT

Your Marrella is officially complete! Check out the gallery on the next page to make sure your piece came out as intended.

THANK YOU SO MUCH FOR ENJOYING MY CROCHET PATTERN BOOK!

Your support of my independent pattern book publication project allows me to continue to pursue my passion of using crochet as a medium to bring silly and obscure prehistoric creatures back from extinction.

When I first started making these creatures, I didn't think anyone would be interested, but I have never been more happy to be wrong about that! Curious prehistory-loving crocheters like you are my favorite kind of people! I am so thankful to have found my tribe in artists like you.

If you enjoyed this book, there will be MANY more like it! I crochet animals from all throughout Earth's history, so if you have a specific period of history that you personally adore, stay tuned! My goal is to write at least one crochet pattern book per geological period, so your favorite is 100% certain to be one of them.

I hope you enjoyed every single one of the crocheted goofballs that you made using my book, and I hope you learned some new techniques and fun animal facts along the way!

ACKNOWLEDGEMENTS

To my sweet love for always brightening my life and being supportive of my talents (even if he thinks I'm just making these silly animals up sometimes!).

To my parents for supporting my craft since childhood.

To my brother for always providing expert constructive feedback on my designs.

To my best friend Gabby for sharing my passion for crochet and getting me through life since age 8.

To my Nannie for passing on the gift of crochet to me.

To my dogs for bringing me joy and reminding me to take breaks and care for myself.

To Mr. Bowen for giving me the gift of graphic design that led to this book being a 100% independent project.

To all of my amazing pattern testers on Instagram who made sure that these patterns were ready for you to enjoy.

To my awesome followers who are always sharing new prehistoric creatures with me.

ABOUT THE AUTHOR

..... Katya McGuane ....

I was born and raised in Southern California with a family of four that always had loving shelter dogs in the house. I have been crocheting since my Texan grandmother (Nannie) taught me how around age 8 or 9. I grew up with her beautiful afghans in my home and I begged her to teach me. Ever since, I have been fascinated by the concept of turning yarn into any form I desire with the power of mathematical formulas.

I have been a lifelong animal lover, and I find that crochet allows me to express this passion in a physically tangible way. I grew up with many animal books that are now weathered by my years of childhood curiosity. I always found myself drawn to the lesser known creatures, which would later inspire my highly specific prehistoric animal crochet niche.

In 2020, I had all the time in the world to refine my crochet craft as well as my pattern-writing abilities. I came up with the name "Katya's Yarn Bois" from a long-standing linguistic joke between my brother and I, where we add the suffix "-boi" to the ends of words to transform them into new nouns. "Yarn boi" is essentially our silly way of referring to anything made of yarn, which in most cases for me is amigurumi.

I also have some background in other art forms, both of which are on display within this book! I have been drawing pretty much my whole life, and over time I've developed a comic book-like digital style.

When I was in high school, I took a graphic design class with the amazing Mr. Bowen, who remains one of my all-time favorite teachers. He taught me design in a very systematic, no-nonsense way that resonated very well with me. I use the things he taught me every day when making content for Katya's Yarn Bois. This book as a whole is the culmination of many of my artistic passions.

Outside of my crochet career, I have a Bachelor's Degree from the University of California, Davis in Chinese Language and Culture with a minor in Linguistics. I find that my minor plays into pattern writing very well. I find it endlessly fascinating that through just a handful of abbreviations and a few descriptive sentences and photos, I can communicate to another person exactly how to make the complex animals that I've designed!

I now reside in the beautiful Midwest where I enjoy the cold weather, rich seasons, and slower pace of life.

I have so many more prehistoric crochet pattern books planned, spanning not just every era of history, but also different animal themes such as prehistoric sharks, stem mammals, etc. If you have a prehistoric animal that you would love to see a pattern for, I am always taking suggestions on Instagram @katyasyarnbois!

EXPLORE MY OTHER PREHISTORIC PATTERNS ONLINE!

I sell all of my crochet patterns individually online on Etsy and Ravelry, and I have a lot more than just Cambrian animals! My Etsy shop organizes all of my creatures by time period for easy browsing. It's a great way to get more prehistoric goodness without having to wait for the next book to come out! Here is just a small handful of examples of fun KYB projects you can add to your queue!

katyasyarnbois.etsy.com/
www.ravelry.com/designers/katya-mcguane

Ammonite (Echioceras)
Jurassic Period
201-145 MYA

Dimetrodon
Permian Period
298-252 MYA

Dunkleosteus
Devonian Period
419-359 MYA

Stethacanthus
Carboniferous Period
359-198 MYA

Inostrancevia
Permian Period
298-252 MYA

Tiktaalik
Devonian Period
419-359 MYA

Spinosaurus
Cretaceous Period
145-66 MYA

Kimberella
Ediacaran Period
635-538 MYA

Doedicurus
Quaternary Period
2.58 MYA - Present

Sea Scorpion
Silurian Period
443-419 MYA

Eretmorhipis
Triassic Period
252-201 MYA

Scutosaurus
Permian Period
298-252 MYA

Aegirocassis
Ordovician Period
485-443 MYA

ETSY

RAVELRY

PATREON

Follow me on Instagram @katyasyarnbois to keep up to date with all of my latest prehistoric animal designs!

GEOLOGIC TIME EXPLAINED

EON	ERA	PERIOD	EPOCH	MYA
Phanerozoic		Quaternary	Holocene	0.0117-0
			Pleistocene	2.58-0.01
		Neogene	Pliocene	5.3-2.58
			Miocene	23-5.3
		Paleogene	Oligocene	33.9-23
			Eocene	56-33.9
			Paleocene	66-56
		Cretaceous		145-66
		Jurassic		201-145
		Triassic		252-201
		Permian		298-252
		Carboniferous		358-398
		Devonian		419-358
		Silurian		443-419
		Ordovician		485-443
		Cambrian		538-485
Proterozoic	Neo-proter.			1B-538
	Meso-proter.			1.6-1B
	Paleo-proter.			2.5-1.6B
Archean	Neoarchean			2.8-2.5B
	Mesoarchean			3.2-2.8B
	Paleoarchean			3.6-3.2B
	Eoarchean			4-3.6B
Hadean				4.6-4B

DIVISIONS OF GEOLOGIC TIME

Eon - Several hundred million to two billion years

Era - Tens to hundreds of millions of years

Period - Millions to tens of millions of years

Epoch - Hundreds of thousands to tens of millions of years

Age - Thousands to millions of years (not shown in the table to the left)

THE EONS

Hadean (HAY-dee-in), 4.6 - 4 BYA - Began with the formation of the Earth 4.5 billion years ago. It is named for Hades, Greek god of the underworld, since the Earth at this time was covered in lava, filled with carbon dioxide and methane, and plagued with frequent extraterrestrial impacts. One of these impacts was with a planet called Thea, which created the moon. The Earth's crust and tectonic plates also formed during this time. Over the course of this eon, many water-bearing comets hit the planet's surface, eventually leading to the formation of our oceans.

Archean (Arr-KEY-in), 4-2.5 BYA - A time when the Earth was almost completely covered in hot oceans much deeper than those of today. The name "Archean" means "ancient" or "original". There was virtually no oxygen at this time. The beginning of this eon overlaps with the Late Heavy Bombardment event, which saw meteor impacts the size of the one that killed the dinosaurs every 15 million years. Life is also believed to have started here, but it was very simple single-celled prokaryotic life. Cyanobacteria were the most dominant species at the time, but various other species existed that were capable of photosynthesis, sulfur-oxidization, and surviving extreme environments. The eon ended with the Huronian Glaciation, a series of around three ice ages where at least one resulted in a "Snowball Earth" where just about the entire surface of the Earth was frozen over.

Proterozoic (PRO-turr-oh-ZOH-ick), 2.5B-538 MYA - A term meaning "early life" in Greek, this eon was when life started growing more complex. Complex single-celled organisms (eukaryotes) and even simple multicellular life forms such as simple sponges developed during this time. This is most likely due to the Great Oxidation Event, which was caused by the release of oxygen as a waste product from photosynthetic organisms. The earliest evidence of fungi is found here. Stromatolites, a rocky formation formed by hardened layers of bacteria, were the most abundant during the Proterozoic eon. The middle of this eon is referred to as the "Boring Billion" by scientists due to its highly stable and seemingly unchanging conditions from 1.8-1 BYA. There was also a Snowball Earth during this eon called the Cryogenian Ice Age. The end of this eon saw the emergence of simple animal life in the Ediacaran Period such as Spriggina, Dickinsonia, and Kimberella.

Phanerozoic (FAN-urr-oh-ZOH-ick), 538 MYA to today - This period encompasses pretty much all of the Earth's complex animal life. Its name means "visible life" in Greek. This temporal boundary was set with the intention of defining the "before and after" of complex animal life, but animal life in the Ediacaran Period (635-538 MYA) was later discovered to have developed in an event we now call the Avalon Explosion. Animal life can even be pushed back to the Tonian Period (1B - 720 MYA) in the form of the sponge *Otavia*. This action-packed eon will be fleshed out in much more detail in the eras, periods, and epochs to follow on the next few pages.

THE ERAS

Paleozoic (PAY-lee-oh-ZOH-ick), 538-252 MYA - This era encompasses the Cambrian, Ordovician, Silurian, Devonian, Carboniferous, and Permian periods and boasts incredible evolutionary and planetary changes. Its name means "early life" in Greek. The Cambrian Period at the start was the largest known explosion of biodiversity, known as the Cambrian Explosion. Arthropods dominated at least the first half of this entire era while soft-bodied chordates and vertebrates did their best to survive.

By the Devonian Period, fish were getting quite large and were beginning to take over apex predator niches, such as in the case of Dunkleosteus. The evolution of amniotic eggs (hard-shelled eggs that can survive on land) developed during this time, which led to the rise of reptiles and amphibians. Towards the end of the era, mammals were beginning to take shape in the form of the stem mammals from the Permian. This era ended with the Late Permian Extinction, which wiped out upwards of 95% of all life on Earth. This made it deadlier than the extinction that wiped out the dinosaurs.

Mesozoic (MEZZ-oh-ZOH-ick), 252-66 MYA - Most know this era best as the age of the dinosaurs, which encompasses the Triassic, Jurassic, and Cretaceous periods. Its name means "middle life" This era started out at the end of the devastating Late Permian Extinction where life was doing its best to slowly recover. At one time, around 95% of all vertebrates living on the land were of a single species: Lystrosaurus! The early Mesozoic recovery saw the proliferation of marine reptiles, the evolution of crocodilians and dinosaurs, and the emergence of the first pterosaurs.

Towards the middle of the Mesozoic, the Earth was more tropical, which came about from the development of seas that broke up the large land masses. Sauropods, stegosaurs, and ammonites were common life forms seen during this time. The end of the Mesozoic saw the age of massive dinosaurs such as Tyrannosaurus Rex and Spinosaurus, just to name a few. The era was punctuated by the K-Pg Extinction (known before as the KT extinction event), with K meaning "Cretaceous" and Pg meaning "Paleogene", as this event marked the end and beginning of these two periods respectively. This event was caused by the Chicxulub impact, named for the town on the Yucutan Peninsula in Mexico where the impact site was discovered. This led to the extinction of all dinosaurs and 75% of all life on Earth, but it would give the mammals their chance to take over.

Cenozoic (SEE-noh-ZOH-ick), 66 MYA to today - This is the era that you and I call home. Its name means "new life" and is characterized by the takeover of mammals, birds, and flowering plants. This is also when our modern continental layout was formed. For the first time ever, mammals could finally grow to large sizes. Giants such as Paraceratherium reached as tall as 16 ft (4.8 m) at the shoulder, whereas before most mammals were lucky to reach the size of a cat.

The beginning of this era was warmer than the present day. The whole planet was hot and humid, and there were forests at the poles with no permanent ice to speak of. The ice caps did not develop until around 35 MYA when Antarctica began to freeze over. Scientists believe that the formation of the Himalayas led to rocks eroding and reacting with CO_2, taking it out of the atmosphere and causing a cooling effect. The Quaternary Period, which we are still in today, is where human beings got their start as dominant life forms on Earth. Our ancestor Australopithecus evolved towards the end of the Neogene Period. Everything currently alive today is considered a Cenozoic animal, including you!

THE PERIODS

Cambrian (CAM-bree-in), 538-485 MYA
- The Cambrian Period, known for its "Cambrian Explosion" of biodiversity, marks the era when animal life really began to kick off. The name "Cambrian" comes from the Latin name for the country of Wales, "Cambria". Most of the fossils from this era were found in the Burgess Shale in British Columbia, or in China's Chengjiang Biota. During this time, most of Earth's above-water land mass was in the southern hemisphere in the Pannotia super continent, but this continent broke apart throughout this period. There were no permanent ice caps, so sea levels were high. As a result, many areas were flooded with warm, shallow waters that made perfect homes for the sea life that was blossoming there. Though there seemed to have been an ebb and flow of water levels, suggesting that ice may have formed and melted periodically.

The only life on the surface of the land at this time was microbial mats. These mats also existed on the sea floor, but burrowing animals destroyed them over time. In the oceans, arthropods dominated. Soft-bodied chordates (the ancestors to vertebrates) existed as well, but they were small and nowhere near the top of the food chain. The period came to an end with the Cambrian-Ordovician Extinction Event, which greatly affected trilobite populations.

Ordovician (Ore-duh-VISH-in), 485-443 MYA
- The Ordovician Period saw the continuation of invertebrate/arthropod dominance with long-shelled cephalopods like Endoceras reigning as an apex predator. Sea Scorpions also came about in the Ordovician. Its name comes from the name of the Welsh tribe, the Ordovices, as many of the fossils from this period were found in North Wales. This is the first time we see evidence of terrestrial plants in the fossil record. Fish with jaws may also have debuted towards the end of this period. Meteorite strikes were quite frequent, striking the Earth as much as 100 times as often as they do today.

The continents were still heavily concentrated in the southern hemisphere of the planet, the largest being Gondwana. The northern hemisphere was dominated by the Panthalassic Ocean. The Early Ordovician was very hot, but it cooled considerably by the Middle Ordovician, resulting in an ice age. The sea levels rose during the warming periods and lowered later on as ice caps formed, which no doubt affected the life evolved for the hot climate.

The period came to a close with the Ordovician-Silurian Extinction Event, which was the second most devastating extinction event in history, second only to the Permian-Triassic Extinction Event.

Silurian (Sih-LURR-ee-in), 443-419 MYA
- The Silurian Period was a relatively short period of time, but it was still full of important evolutionary milestones. Its name comes from the Celtic tribe of Wales, the Silures, a nod to where the fossils of this period were found. This was the age of the jawed fish, which would greatly diversify into such groups as the placoderms (ex. Dunkleosteus), lobe- and ray-finned fish, and the acanthodians which were a precursor to the cartilaginous fish that would eventually give us sharks. This was also when the first "forests" showed up in the form of large fungi pillars called Prototaxites that could reach up to 29 ft (8.8 m) tall.

Three of the smaller continents from the Ordovician (Siberia, Laurentia, and Avalonia) merged together to create another supercontinent: Euramerica. The climate also fluctuated quite a bit, entering a high-CO_2 greenhouse period where the ice caps of the Ordovician melted away and produced many shallow seas. There were also many violent storms.

Life on land began to diversify quite a bit. Vascular plants, which are plants that can carry food and water through its tissues, came onto the scene with Cooksonia being one of the earliest specimens. Arthropods also ventured onto the land, including millipedes, centipedes, and trigonotarbids (a primitive arachnid). The Silurian Period's end wasn't punctuated by any particular disaster, but the fossil record shows a defined line between it and the following Devonian Period, known as the Silurian-Devonian Boundary.

Devonian (Duh-VOH-nee-in), 419-358 MYA -
This is the time where life on the land began to truly proliferate. Its name comes from the county of Devon in England where early debates about the dates of this period took place. Plants and forests spread across the land, creating brand new ecosystems. Plants evolved leaves, roots, and seeds. Our ancestor Tiktaalik took its first steps on the land as well. The oceans were dominated by the placoderms (armored fish), with Dunkleosteus being the apex predator of the time. It is often referred to as "The Age of Fishes". Primitive sharks also began to diversify in form (the Carboniferous is when they really get interesting). Ammonites got their start in the Devonian as well.

The Devonian was warm, with relatively little permanent ice compared to today. The equator was dry and arid, and the surface of the water was around 86° F (30° C). The growing forests of the Devonian pulled carbon out of the atmosphere to use in their tissues, leading to a cooling effect (temperatures dropped by 9°F or 5°C). Corals and sponges thrived in these cooler temperatures, and their extinction may have caused temperatures to go back up towards the end of the Devonian.

The period came to an end with the Late Devonian Extinction, which was a series of extinction events towards the end of the period. Most of the species affected were sea creatures. 96% of vertebrates disappeared, and the placoderms died out completely, making it one of the five big extinction events. Scientists debate over whether tetrapods on the land were relatively unaffected or nearly wiped out.

Carboniferous (CAR-buh-NIFF-urr-iss), 358-298 MYA -
This period is when amphibian life flourished. It is named after the prolific coal beds discovered from this era, with "carboniferous" meaning "coal-bearing". Contrary to popular belief, the energy we burn does not come from dinosaurs, but from plant matter that was compressed into coal. This was able to happen because microscopic life capable of breaking down dead life forms had not evolved yet, so dead plants piled up in the fossil record. This period is typically split into two distinct halves: the Pennsylvanian and the Mississippian.

Known as "The Age of Amphibians", we see many large amphibian species developing. Since vertebrate life on land was still fairly fresh out of the ocean, it was still heavily dependent on the water, especially when it came time to breed. Thankfully, the Earth was rich with swamps and rainforests that supported semi-aquatic life. The high levels of oxygen also allowed bugs to reach scary sizes. The ancient Pulmonoscorpius was as long as a grown man's arm! The high levels of oxygen had a cooling side effect that caused a glaciation for a while. This high oxygen also made thunderstorms much more dangerous, as lightning strikes could ignite fires more easily.

Towards the end of this period, the rainforests began dying out (referred to as the Carboniferous Rainforest Collapse). This saw a transition from warm jungle climates to a cool and dry one, which caused an extinction event for the creatures that had evolved for the former conditions. The vertebrates that were heading towards a more reptilian form complete with hard-shelled eggs would adapt to these conditions far better than the amphibians.

Permian (PURR-mee-in), 298-252 MYA - This period is when we see the precursors to mammals arise, occupying a curious "middle ground" between reptiles and mammals (called stem mammals). The period is named after the Perm region of Russia where many of these fossils were found. The two groups that came to dominate this era were the synapsids and the sauropsids (a group that includes the precursors to reptiles as well as birds). Synapsids are defined by the single hole in their skulls behind the eye, where as diapsids (such as dinosaurs) had two. This gave them a stronger bite force.

All of the major continents at this time were joined together as Pangaea. Land masses as large as Pangaea don't let in as much rainfall in the center, so deserts were common. Plants with seeds protected by hard covers (gymnosperms) did well in this dry environment, which led to the spread of Earth's first modern trees. The Permian started out relatively cool and got warmer and dryer over time. On the coasts, however, rainforests persisted. Tall mountains blocked rain from coming inland and caused distinct climate divides, known as the "rain shadow effect".

The Permian came to an end with the most devastating extinction event in Earth's history: the Permian-Triassic Extinction Event. Around 90-95% of all ocean life and 70% of terrestrial life died out, a devastation that would take 30 million years to recover from. This is also the only mass extinction of insects that we have record of. One major factor was the flooding of the Earth with magma over the course of thousands of years, which caused a significant greenhouse effect as CO_2 was expelled. The oceans may also have vented hydrogen sulfide gas, which was deadly to most of the sea life at that time.

Triassic (Try-ASS-ick), 252-201 MYA - This time period's name means "three groups", a reference to the three distinct layers of rock

formations that defined this era. Life on Triassic Earth started with a labored crawl, as living things during this time were still recovering from the worst mass extinction in Earth's history. The hot, dry climate of the Permian persisted, with inland temperatures hitting as high as 145°F (62°C). However, Pangaea was starting to break up, allowing for moisture to reach the inland parts of the supercontinent and create humid environments once again.

The earliest dinosaur species developed towards the end of this period, as did pterosaurs and the ancestors of modern crocodiles. Marine reptiles also diversified during this time, including the first plesiosaurs. Early turtles also found their start here. Mammal-like reptiles, known as therapsids, were continuing to evolve and diversify. Lystrosaurus (a therapsid) in the early Triassic made up around 95% of all land vertebrates!

This period also ended with a major mass extinction (Triassic-Jurassic Extinction Event). It was particularly harsh in the oceans, but many land animals were also significantly affected. The cause isn't known for sure, but there were massive volcanic eruptions around this time, which could have changed the atmosphere that life at the time was used to. One of these eruptions was one of the largest since the Earth's crust first hardened into place during the Hadean Eon. This extinction event left many niches open, allowing dinosaurs to rapidly diversify and eventually take over in the Jurassic.

Jurassic (Jurr-ASS-ick), 201-145 MYA - This period was named for the Jura Mountains, a forested mountain range along the border of France and Switzerland. Further, Jura comes from the Celtic word for "wooded mountain". As you would be correct to assume, many fossils from this period were discovered in this area. During this time, dinosaurs took over as the dominant group on Earth.

The first birds, crabs, and modern lizards appeared, and early mammals began to diversify. Marine reptiles continued to dominate the oceans as modern sharks took shape, and pterosaurs took over the skies.

Pangaea broke apart into Laurasia and Gondwana, slowly forming the still very narrow North Atlantic Ocean. North and South America separated and created the Caribbean Seaway. Temperatures were generally quite a bit warmer than today (+5-10°C), which allowed for forests to grow at the poles, though rainforests were likely rare or even non-existent.

The dinosaurs that thrived during this time included sauropods (ex. Diplodocus & Brachiosaurus), Allosaurus, Stegosaurus, and Iguanadon. The Jurassic did not end quite as drastically as other periods. It is likely that though many species didn't make it to the Cretaceous, they were replaced by other species in a sort of "changing of the guard".

Cretaceous (Krih-TAY-shuss), 145-66 MYA -
The name "Cretaceous" contains the Latin word "Creta", meaning "chalk", referring to the chalky limestone found in the fossil layers of this time. This time period is a favorite amongst paleontology lovers because this is when dinosaurs reached their peak. Flowers also evolved during this time, which took over as the dominant plant group. Ammonites and marine reptiles also continued going strong.

Pangaea was completely broken up into today's continents, though they were in very different positions at this time. North America was also cut in half by the Western Interior Seaway. The climate was still relatively warm, but the high and low latitudes did experience some snowfall. There were also wet environments that were absent during the Jurassic.

Many favorites of dino lovers called the Cretaceous home, including Tyrannosaurus Rex, Triceratops, Velociraptor, Ankylosaurus, and the massive flying Quetzalcoatlus. This period ended with the famous KT (now K-Pg) Extinction Event, which was caused by a massive meteorite impact known as the Chicxulub impact crater. The crater is believed to be around 120 miles (200 km) across and 12 miles (20 km) deep!

Paleogene (PAY-lee-oh-jeen), 66-23 MYA -
This period's name means "ancient-born" in Greek, as it is the earliest period of the Cenozoic era that would see the rise of the mammals. For as long as they were living in the shadow of the dinosaurs, mammals stayed relatively small and simple, but following the K-Pg Extinction Event, many ecological niches were now ripe for the taking.

The Paleogene started out with a harsh but relatively short "impact winter", a phenomenon caused by significant meteorite impacts. Once the metaphorical dust settled, temperatures stabilized and warmed, though they would fluctuate here and there. The Himalayas formed during the Paleogene as India crashed into Asia, Africa pushed up against Europe to create the Mediterranean Sea, and North and South America joined up again at the Isthmus of Panama. The Western Interior Seaway also drained out of the middle of North America.

Notable animals of this period include the massive Paraceratherium (a 16 ft/5 m tall creature that looked like a hornless rhino giraffe), the fearsome predator Andrewsarchus, the Titanoboa, and Pakicetus (the hooved land animal that would eventually evolve into whales!). The end of this period is marked by a significant change in climate conditions. Temperatures rose and CO^2 levels dropped, leading to an iceless Arctic with a lush forest.

Neogene (NEE-oh-geen), 23-2.58 MYA - The name of this period means "recently born", which references the rise of modern animal groups and ecosystems during this time. Many of the species alive during this time look quite familiar, as they would be the precursors to our modern animals that we know today. Humanity also got its footing towards the very end of this period in the form of Homo Habilis.

The continental map of the Neogene looks almost identical to our current one, save some land bridges and other minor differences. The period fluctuated between cool periods and warming optimums, including the Middle Miocene Climatic Optimum and the Pliocene Thermal Maximum. The period ended with the Ice Age, which persists to this day.

The Paleogene was home to such creatures as Megalodon, Deinotherium, Thylacosmilus, mammoths, and woolly rhinos (I have crocheted all but Megalodon at the time of writing this book!). The division between the Neogene and the following Quaternary is actually disputed by scientists. Some believe that we should consider the present day to be a continuation of the Neogene, while others believe that the glaciation period warrants a separation. Additionally, since the Cenozoic is the most recent, its fossil record is the most rich, so it is much easier to draw dividing lines into smaller time periods such as epochs and ages. This fact also causes some dispute on how to separate the Cenozoic periods.

Quaternary (KWOT-urr-nair-ee), 2.58 MYA-Present - You know this period well, as you are living in it right now! There are two epochs (the Pleistocene and Holocene), but some are arguing for there to be an Anthropocene (the Age of Humans), whose hypothetical dates range as far back as the Agricultural revolution 12-15,000 years ago to as recently as the 20th century (the Atomic Age). The 2.58 MYA date encompasses the timeline of human species

that are recognizable to us as human.

During this time, land bridges rose and fell, which allowed humans to reach new lands. Two notable ones were the one that connected the British Islands to mainland Europe, and the Bering Strait that connected Russia to Alaska. Michigan's Great Lakes also formed during the Quaternary. This period is also defined by its Ice Age, which we are still in due to our frozen poles.

Some significant extinct Quaternary animals include the Woolly Mammoth, Gigantopithecus, the Sabertooth Tiger, Glyptodons, and Megatherium. Everything currently alive today is also in this category, including you and I! This period is ongoing and will likely persist for many millions of years before the next one begins.

THE EPOCHS OF THE CENOZOIC

Paleocene (PAY-lee-oh-seen), 66-56 MYA - The Paleocene was the first epoch of both the Paleogene Period and the Cenozoic Era. Its name means "recently ancient". It came right at the end of the K-Pg Extinction Event and is defined by its explosion of mammal diversity in the absence of the dinosaurs. The climate was warm and tropical with temperate poles. The animals at the time consisted of small rodent-like mammals, giant flightless predatory birds, and a still diverse but much smaller array of reptiles including turtles, crocodiles, lizards, and snakes like Titanoboa.

Eocene (EE-oh-seen), 56-33.9 MYA - The Eocene spans the transition from an extreme hot climate to a very cold one. Its name means "new dawn". The border between the Paleocene and Eocene epochs is the Paleocene-Eocene Thermal Maximum, which was the warm end of this epoch.

It ended with the Eocene-Oligocene Extinction Event, which was likely triggered by the onset of the Late Cenozoic Ice Age. This period saw the proliferation of large and fearsome mammalian predators such as Andrewsarchus and bear dogs (amphicyonids). Many ancestors to some familiar modern faces also evolved in the Eocene, such as horses, elephants, bats, and even primates.

Oligocene (Oh-LIG-oh-seen), 33.9-23 MYA

- The Oligocene was a time of transition between the warm and tropical world of the Paleogene and modern climate conditions. Its name means "few new" because of the scarcity of mollusk life forms. During this time, Antarctica was becoming more and more isolated and was beginning to freeze. Ancestors of such animals as rhinos, deer, camels, bears, dogs, and raccoons came onto the scene during the Oligocene. The massive Paraceratherium also existed during this time (one of Earth's largest land mammals!).

Miocene (MY-oh-seen), 23-5.3 MYA

- The Miocene was the first epoch of the Neogene Period. Its name means "less recent" or "smaller new", which refers to the fact that it had "18% fewer modern marine invertebrates than the Pliocene" (Lyell). The entire period was on a downward slide in temperature, heading towards the ice age of today. Africa and the Arabian Peninsula merged with Eurasia, which allowed for animal species to mix around on the new land mass. During this time, the Mediterranean Sea almost completely evaporated away, but it was thankfully refilled by a flood, marking the end of the epoch. The human and chimp evolutionary branches split here as primates diversified. Over a hundred species of ape have been documented! Whales were also recognizable during this time and were highly diverse by today's standards. Other new species at the time included otters, beavers, bears, more modern canines, and even red pandas.

Pliocene (PLY-oh-seen), 5.3-2.58 MYA

- A relatively short epoch, the Pliocene marked yet another phase of movement from warm to cool, with its end at the start of the Pleistocene glaciations of the Ice Age. Its name means "more recent". The Earth's climate was also drying and becoming more seasonal. Animals such as chalicotheres and the three-toed horses went extinct and hoofed animals of all kinds saw a recession in their populations. Proboscideans (elephant-like animals) and rodents, however, saw a population boom. We also see large glyptodonts, short-faced bears, and ground sloths thriving in this epoch. Human evolution was also on its way, with Australopithecus and Homo Habilis evolving throughout this time period.

Pleistocene (PLISE-toh-seen), 258 MYA-11,700 YA

- This is the period of time that people are referring to when they say "The Ice Age". Its name means "most new", as it is the most recent epoch before the one that we are currently living in (the Holocene). Though we are currently living in an Ice Age, the permanent ice sheets during this time reached far further south than they do now. Some maps show the Laurentide Ice Sheet of North America completely covering American states like New York and Wisconsin! With so much water occupied by glaciers, the sea levels were around 390 ft (120 m) lower than they are today in some places. The measurements of the ice sheets are even more awe-inspiring: continental ice sheets measured anywhere from 4,900-9,800 ft (1,500 - 3,000 m) thick! By this point, Antarctica was the icy wasteland that we know it to be today.

Animals of this time period will be familiar to many: woolly mammoths, the giant sloth Megatherium, reindeer, woolly rhinos, sabertooth tigers, and Megalania (a large monitor lizard). Human beings achieved their anatomically-modern forms and began using fire, weapons, clothing, and other intelligent tools and processes.

The Pleistocene Epoch is punctuated by an abrupt cooling period known as the Younger Dryas. There is a controversial theory (the Younger Dryas Impact Theory) that suggests the Earth was struck by a comet or other extraterrestrial body around 11,700 years ago in an event that changed the landscape of the planet very rapidly. Many point to the existence of great flood myths in a diverse array of cultures as evidence that something catastrophic happened around this time. There is still much heated scientific debate on the validity of this theory, as many key things have yet to be convincingly proven. There are multiple other theories on what led to the drastic changes in climate, including changes in the flow of ocean currents or volcanic activity. There is still much research to be done on the topic!

Holocene (HAWL-oh-seen), 11,700 YA-Pres.
- This period needs little explaining, as it's the one we're in right now! Its name means "whole new", meaning that this epoch is entirely new and unique from everything else that came before it. It is a highly anthropocentric epoch, as its beginning is timed with the first (that we know of) agricultural revolution. This is the modern Earth as we know it, both continentally and climatically for the most part. All animals alive today are considered Holocene animals. If you'd like to know more about the Holocene, you'd be better off simply studying modern zoology and geography!

NOTE

I am by no means an expert on any of these topics, this information was simply gleaned from online research with academic sources available to me as a layman. I did my absolute best to get accurate information from accredited sources and to avoid making any statements or claims that I could not directly back up with a source. There may be some inaccuracies here and there, so I wouldn't recommend using these pages to study for your upcoming natural history test, but simply to satisfy your curiosity of prehistory on a surface level! If you find this content fascinating, I highly encourage you to pursue further knowledge on your own accord!

HOW TO CARE FOR YOUR CROCHETED CREATIONS

MILD SOILING

If your amigurumi plush is only mildly dirty, you can clean it by hand. If there is dry debris, try to dust off as much as you can with your hands. Then, grab a wet wash cloth and gently wipe at the area until the remaining dirt is gone. Let any remaining moisture air dry in a dry and well-ventilated place to prevent any mildew development.

HEAVY SOILING

If your amigurumi is dirty enough that a wet rag is not enough to do the job, it may be in need of a deeper clean. Fill up a sink with water and wool wash (or just a mild soap if you don't have any) and gently dip your amigurumi in the water and massage the dirt out of the fabric. If your amigurumi is made from machine-washable yarn, you may be able to put it in your washing machine on a gentle wash setting with cold water. Then air-dry the piece in a cool, dry, and well-ventilated area.

CARING FOR DIFFERENT TYPES OF YARN

If your project is made with wool or other natural fibers, machine washing may put your piece at risk of "felting" the fabric, especially if hot water is used. This means that the stitches become so agitated that the fabric turns into a big piece of felt and the stitch texture disappears. In this case, avoid machine washing unless absolutely necessary, Do so with cold water and a gentle wash cycle if you must. Keep out of the dryer, the heat can cause shrinkage in some yarn types! Air dry is the safest bet for amigurumi. When in doubt, always check the yarn label for washing instructions!

MAKING YOUR PROJECTS CHILD-FRIENDLY

Young children oftentimes find the most innovative ways to get hurt with seemingly harmless items! Thankfully there are a few ways you can make sure your amigurumi isn't a risk to a child's safety.

CHOKING HAZARDS

One of the biggest risks, despite having "safety " in the name, is actually plastic safety eyes. Even if they are secured firmly in very tight stitches, years of play can loosen stitches around eyes and cause them to fall out. You can remedy this by instead crocheting simple circles and securely sewing them down. You can simply ch 2 and sc 6 in the 2nd ch from hook, cut and tie off, and use the tail to sew it onto your project. If you need bigger eyes, you can always add another round or so of 6 equidistant increases. Gluing of any kind is not advised. Kids can also get fingers stuck and twisted in crochet stitches as well if they are not tight enough, so crocheting as tightly as possible can reduce this risk. Make sure you're always monitoring the toy for any ends that may come loose from play.

CHOOSING THE RIGHT MATERIALS

Anyone who still has their favorite childhood stuffed animal will be able to tell you that children get them very dirty! You will want to make sure you make your amigurumis with machine-washable yarn so that it can withstand years of baths. You should also stuff toys with standard Polyfil stuffing. Don't use weighted beads, as these can sneak their way out of the stitches and become choking hazards. You may want to omit stem wire as well just to avoid potential poke-through. However if you make sure to bend the sharp end over itself to give it a more rounded end before inserting it into the piece, you may not have any issues with poke-through.

TIPS TO IMPROVE YOUR AMIGURUMI PROJECTS!

INVISIBLE DECREASES

There are several different ways to make decreases, most of which leave behind a clear indication in your work that a decrease was made there. The best way to decrease in a way that's almost indistinguishable from the rest of your stitches is as follows:

Insert into the first stitch, yarn over, and pull up a loop (Fig. 1). Then insert into the second stitch and yarn over (Fig. 2), and then pull directly through the other two loops on your hook WITHOUT stopping to yarn over again (Fig. 3 & 4).

The only time you should not do this is if you need to make another stitch into the same stitch that you just ended the decrease in. In my patterns, this would occur in a 2/3 inc or 2/3 dec. This is because this style of decrease is finished off like a slst, and it is impossible to work more than one slst into the same stitch.

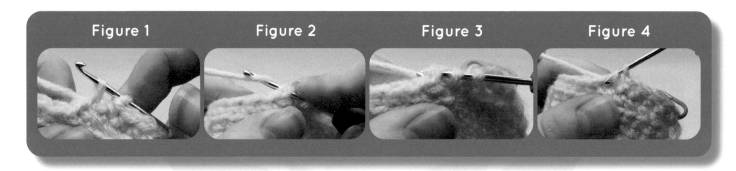

| Figure 1 | Figure 2 | Figure 3 | Figure 4 |

CROCHETING BACKWARDS

The name of this technique sounds absurd, but it will be a game changer in making your amigurumi look sleek! Sometimes in amigurumi, we have to work in rows to shape certain pieces, most notably when working in short rows to change the direction of a piece. The texture of crochet fabric worked in rows is noticeably different than fabric worked in rounds, and this can look rather unsightly in amigurumi. The solution is to crochet "backwards" on the rows where you are "inside out" (i.e. working on the wrong side of the round).

Insert your hook through the BACK side of the stitch (Fig. 1). If you normally yarn under in your amigurumi, you will yarn over (Fig. 2) and pull up a loop (Fig. 3), and vice versa if you like to yarn over. Then, yarn under (Fig. 4) and pull through the loops (this yarn under is regardless of whether you do YU or YO typically).

I am a YU/YO crocheter (explained in next tip), so Figure 2 is following the "if you yarn under when working forward, then yarn over when working backwards" rule. This technique takes some practice to solidify the muscle memory, but it's well worth it!

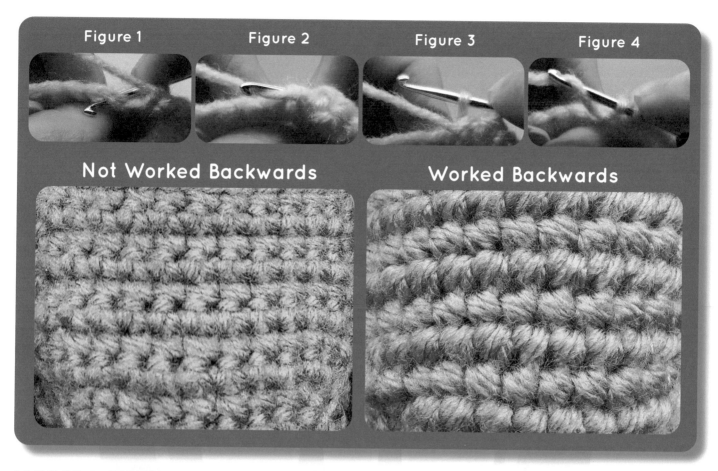

Figure 1   **Figure 2**   **Figure 3**   **Figure 4**

Not Worked Backwards   **Worked Backwards**

YARN UNDER VS. YARN OVER

Single crochet stitches can be worked in 4 different ways. A sc stitch contains two instances where a loop is made and pulled through a stitch or loops, which gives two different instances where a crocheter can either "yarn over (YO)" or "yarn under (YU)". The combinations below are structured so that the first two letters of the acronym refer to how the first loop is done, and the second two letters refer to how the second loop is done.

YO/YO: The standard method in crochet (V-shaped stitches, looks better with chenille yarn)

YU/YO: Used to make tighter X-shaped stitches that have a clean look

YO/YU: Square single crochet (a lesser-known stitch used often in tapestry crochet to create a perfectly square-shaped stitch, makes complex color work look more like a clean pixel grid)

YU/YU: Can make stitches even tighter than YUYO, also makes fabric denser.

Starting with YU can make your stitches slant less from round to round, so this may result in alignment discrepancies when following patterns sometimes, though most times the difference is negligible. Note the purple lines on each photo (p. 170); this shows how much the stitches shift as you work when using each of the different techniques (these pieces are done right-handed). FYI, **ALL Katya's Yarn Bois patterns are worked in YU/YO!**

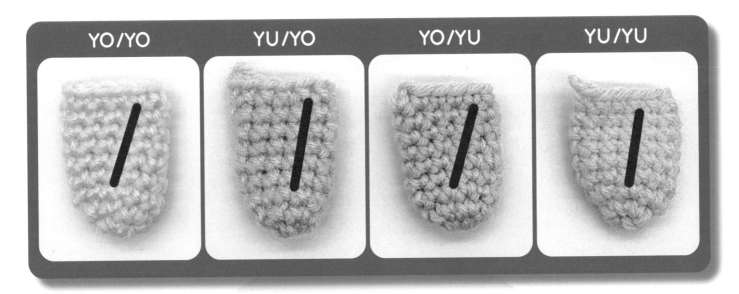

SMOOTHER COLOR CHANGES

When working in spiral rounds, it can be quite tough to get color changes to not look so harsh and stair-steppy. There are some techniques that look quite nice, but require the working of an entire round of slip stitches and then a round of sc stitches behind them in the same round that the slsts were worked into. This isn't always possible to do when trying to follow a pattern exactly, and can be a lot of extra work in larger rounds.

Instead, if you simply make the very first stitch of the new color a slst instead of a sc, it will look much less blocky. You will then work into it like a normal sc stitch in the next round. It's not flawless, but it's much easier and more convenient than other techniques and will not interfere with following patterns. If the first stitch of the new color round is an increase, simply work it as two sc stitches. Not only do you not need to do so to get it to look right, but the nature of a slst makes it impossible to work another stitch after it into the same stitch!

Without slst   With slst

SMOOTHER SHORT ROWS

Short rows are when you work a series of rows in an amigurumi piece where each is fewer stitches than the last, creating a stair step shape. This allows you to change the direction of a piece of amigurumi, and it has virtually unlimited potential shaping uses.

When returning to rounds after a series of short rows, the edges of the rows can leave an unsightly bumpiness. A very easy fix to this issue is to not ch 1 when you turn (i.e. turn without chaining). This will cause the first stitches of those rows to slope downward with the flow of the new round orientation, making it look much smoother!

Additionally, I find it also helps to smooth things out and reduce gaps if you make decreases in the last stitch of the stair step and in the base of that same stitch on the row below (this is when you are working DOWN the stair steps). To put it another way, just before the first stitch of that next short row "stair step", there is a stitch that was already worked into by the last stitch of the short row directly above it (Fig. 1 on p. 172). I call these **root spaces** for explanation's sake. This will be the second stitch of your decrease. Since you are making this decrease in a stitch that does not count towards the round count, it will not affect your count.

When you are working UP the stair steps, you will finish all of the legal stitches in the stair step, then make a decrease that starts in the root space that sits at the base of the next stair step and ends in the first stitch of that next stair step up above. After this decrease, you will continue in the next available stitch of the stair step.

GAPLESS JOINS

When joining two (or more) separate pieces together into a single round, there is often complaint that the spot where the pieces were joined has unsightly gaps. With this technique, that problem will be a thing of the past! It involves making decreases that work into "non-legal" stitches.

I use the term "legal" stitch to refer to any stitch that is counted towards the round/row count. A "non-legal" stitch is a space somewhere in the round/row that is NOT one of these legal stitches. In this specific instance, the non-legal stitch will be a stitch that has already been worked into that sits at the base of the last stitch that was worked in that round (Fig. 1). This will be referred to as the **"root space"**, and the decreases made in them will be called **"root decreases"**. Feel free to use the invisible decrease technique here!

Your first root decrease will start in the last legal stitch made in Piece 1 before hopping over to Piece 2, and it will end in the root space of Piece 2 (Fig. 2). Then crochet all the way around Piece 2 until you get to its very last legal stitch. The second root decrease will start in this last legal stitch of Piece 2 and will end in the root space directly below it, also still in Piece 2 (Fig. 3). Your third and final root decrease will come directly after the second one. It will start in the root space of Piece 1 that was worked into previously by the first root decrease, and it will end in the first available legal stitch of Piece 1 (Fig. 4). Then, finish your round. Make sure all of these decreases are tight to fully eliminate gaps!

Once you finish off this round, your join is complete! These decreases will have no effect on your round count since half of the decrease is worked into a space that did not count as a legal stitch to begin with. If you find that your round count has dropped during this round, check back to make sure that all of your decreases were worked in one legal stitch and one root space and not two legal stitches. You can also use this in any pattern you follow without worry that it will throw off your piece from the pattern's intention.

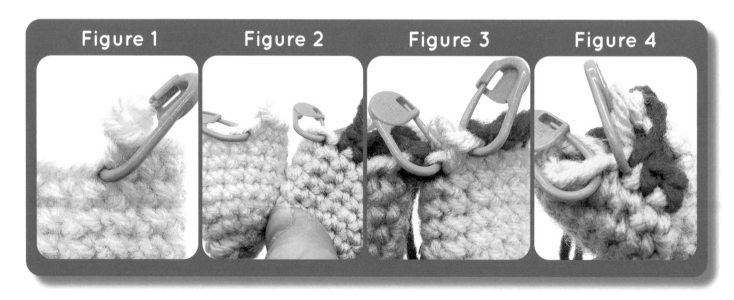

Figure 1   Figure 2   Figure 3   Figure 4

STUFFING YOUR PIECE PROPERLY

Stuffing is an aspect of crochet that many people don't even realize has a proper method and technique to it! I must confess that for the longest time, I used to stuff my animals so tightly that they felt like NERF footballs, but then I learned this trick!

Take a piece of stuffing and pull it apart over and over until you are left with light, fluffy clouds. Then, stuff your piece with one small quantity at a time, making sure to fill in every nook and cranny. By fluffing the stuffing and only using a small amount at a time, you are able to evenly fill your piece without leaving empty gaps. Unfluffed stuffing has a more rigid and unforgiving form, so you may find yourself trying to put in more and more stuffing to fill the ever-forming gaps, and before you know it you've made your piece hard as a rock!

As an added bonus, stuffing with light, fluffy stuffing leads to less stuffing being used, which will save you money in the long run. And if you're willing to pay a little extra, there also exists "Luxury Down Alternative" fiber fill, which is light and silky and does not need to be pulled apart. It is definitely worth the money!

COMING UP NEXT!

..... Permian Period Vol. 1! ....

Katya's Yarn Bois's next crochet pattern book will focus on the Permian Period (298-252 MYA). It will feature 10 unique creature designs ranging from intermediate to advanced difficulty. If you were able to make your way through the patterns of this book, you will be more than ready for this one!

Check out the official line-up (with one surprise design!) here! If you want to be kept up to date with the production of this book, be sure to follow me on Instagram @ katyasyarnbois. Or if you just cannot wait for one of these specific patterns, be sure to check me out on Etsy or Ravelry to find the individual patterns for each of these creatures! (QR code links to both of these websites can be found on page 155)

COTYLORHYNCHUS

DIMETRODON

DIPLOCAULUS

ESTEMMENOSUCHUS

HELICOPRION

INOSTRANCEVIA

PLATYHYSTRIX

PRIONOSUCHUS

SCUTOSAURUS

???

ACADEMIC SOURCES

Anomalocaris

Briggs DE (1979). "Anomalocaris, the largest known Cambrian arthropod". Palaeontology. 22 (3): 631–664.

Hagadorn JW (August 2009). "Taking a Bite out of Anomalocaris" (PDF). In Smith MR, O'Brien LJ, Caron J (eds.). Abstract Volume. International Conference on the Cambrian Explosion (Walcott 2009). Toronto, Ontario, Canada: The Burgess Shale Consortium (published 31 July 2009).

Saleh F, Qi C, Buatois LA, Mángano MG, Paz M, Vaucher R, et al. (March 2022). "The Chengjiang Biota inhabited a deltaic environment". Nature Communications. 13 (1): 1569.

"Senses. Insect eyes". Insects and Spiders of the World. Volume 8: Scorpion fly - Stinkbug. New York: Marshall Cavendish. 2003. p. 459

Usami Y (January 2006). "Theoretical study on the body form and swimming pattern of Anomalocaris based on hydrodynamic simulation". Journal of Theoretical Biology. 238 (1): 11–7.

Duplapex

Izquierdo-López, Alejandro; Caron, Jean-Bernard (December 2022). "The problematic Cambrian arthropod Tuzoia and the origin of mandibulates revisited". Royal Society Open Science. Vol. 9, Issue 12.

Haikouichthys

"The Cambrian: Vertebrates". Archived from the original on 2009-04-29. Retrieved 2024-04-12.

Fandom, Inc. (n.d.). Haikouichthys. Walking With Wikis. https://walkingwith.fandom.com/wiki/Haikouichthys

Haikouichthys. Prehistoric Wildlife. (n.d.). https://www.prehistoric-wildlife.com/species/h/haikouichthys.html

Shu, D. G.; Conway Morris, S.; Han, J.; Zhang, Z. F.; Yasui, K.; Janvier, P.; Chen, L.; Zhang, X. L.; Liu, J. N.; Li, Y.; Liu, H. -Q. (2003), "Head and backbone of the Early Cambrian vertebrate Haikouichthys", Nature, 421 (6922): 526–529

Wikimedia Foundation. (2024, March 10). Haikouichthys. Wikipedia. https://en.wikipedia.org/wiki/Haikouichthys

Hallucigenia

Duhaime-Ross, A. (2015, June 24). After 50 years, scientists discover head of the insane hallucigenia "worm." The Verge. https://www.theverge.com/2015/6/24/8838169/hallucigenia-worm-fossil-nature-study-2015

Gonzalez, Sebastian Adolfo Osio (18 November 2023). "Attack on Titan Finale: What is the Hallucigenia Worm?". DualShockers. Retrieved 12 April 2024.

Liu, Jianni; Dunlop, Jason A. (15 March 2014). "Cambrian lobopodians: A review of recent progress in our understanding of their morphology and evolution". Palaeogeography, Palaeoclimatology, Palaeoecology. Cambrian Bioradiation. 398: 4–15.

Marrella

Bottjer, David J.; Etter, Walter; Hagadorn, James W.; Tang, Carol M. (2002). Exceptional Fossil Preservation: A unique view on the evolution of marine life. Columbia University Press. p. 70.

García-Bellido, Diego & Collins, Desmond. (2006). A new study of Marrella splendens (Arthropoda, Marrellomorpha) from the Middle Cambrian Burgess Shale, British Columbia, Canada. Canadian Journal of Earth Sciences. 43. 721-742.

Whittington, H. B. (1971). "Redescription of Marrella splendens (Trilobitoidea) from the Burgess Shale, Middle Cambrian, British Columbia" (PDF). Bulletin – Geological Survey of Canada. Geological Survey of Canada. 209: 1–24.

Opabinia

Walcott, C. D. 1912. Middle Cambrian Branchiopoda, Malacostraca, Trilobita and Merostomata. Smithsonian Miscellaneous Collections, 57: 145-228.

Whittington, H. B. (June 1975). "The enigmatic animal Opabinia regalis, Middle Cambrian Burgess Shale, British Columbia". Philosophical Transactions of the Royal Society B. 271 (910): 1–43 271.

Pambdelurion

Budd, G. E. (1997). "Stem group arthropods from the Lower Cambrian Sirius Passet fauna of North Greenland". In Fortey, R. A.; Thomas, R. H. (eds.). Arthropod Relationships. Dordrecht: Springer Netherlands. pp. 125–138.

Vinther, Jakob; Porras, Luis; Young, Fletcher J.; Budd, Graham E.; Edgecombe, Gregory D. (2016). "The mouth apparatus of the Cambrian gilled lobopodian Pambdelurion whittingtoni". Palaeontology. 59 (6): 841–849.

Young, Fletcher J.; Vinther, Jakob (2017). "Onychophoran-like myoanatomy of the Cambrian gilled lobopodian Pambdelurion whittingtoni". Palaeontology. 60 (1): 27–54.

Pikaia

Mallatt, Jon; Holland, Nicholas (2013). "Pikaia gracilens Walcott: Stem Chordate, or Already Specialized in the Cambrian?". Journal of Experimental Zoology Part B: Molecular and Developmental Evolution. 320 (4): 247–271.

Striedter, Georg F.; Northcutt, R. Glenn (2020). Brains Through Time: A Natural History of Vertebrates. Oxford University Press. p. 70.

Walcott, Charles D. (1911). "Cambrian Geology and Paleontology II: No.5--Middle Cambrian Annelids" (PDF). Smithsonian Miscellaneous Collections. 57 (5): 109–144.

Wilt, Fred H.; Killian, Christopher E.; Livingston, Brian T. (2003). "Development of calcareous skeletal elements in invertebrates". Differentiation. 71 (4–5): 237–250.

Sidneyia

Bruton D. L. 1981 The arthropod Sidneyia inexpectans, Middle Cambrian, Burgess Shale, British Columbia Phil. Trans. R. Soc. Lond. B295619–653

Zacaï, Axelle; Vannier, Jean; Lerosey-Aubril, Rudy (2016). "Reconstructing the diet of a 505-million-year-old arthropod: Sidneyia inexpectans from the Burgess Shale fauna". Arthropod Structure & Development. 45 (2): 200–220.

Waptia

Jean-Bernard Caron & Donald A. Jackson (2006). "Taphonomy of the Greater Phyllopod Bed community, Burgess Shale". PALAIOS. 21 (5): 451–465.

Jean-Bernard Caron & Jean Vannier (2016). "Waptia and the diversification of brood care in early arthropods". Current Biology. 26 (1): 69–74.

Parks, Douglas R.; DeMallie, Raymond J. (1992). "Sioux, Assiniboine, and Stoney Dialects: A Classification". Anthropological Linguistics. 34 (1/4): 233–255.

Wiwaxia

Conway Morris, S. (1985). "The Middle Cambrian metazoan Wiwaxia corrugata (Matthew) from the Burgess Shale and Ogygopsis Shale, British Columbia, Canada". Philosophical Transactions of the Royal Society of London B. 307 (1134): 507–582.

Smith, M.R. (2014). "Ontogeny, morphology and taxonomy of the soft-bodied Cambrian 'mollusc' Wiwaxia". Palaeontology. 57 (1): 215 229.

Hadean Eon

Cohen, Kim (October 2022). "New edition of the Chart - 2022-10". International Commission on Stratigraphy. Retrieved 27 April 2024.

Korenaga, J (2021). "Was There Land on the Early Earth?". Life. 11 (11): 1142.

Archean Eon

Borgeat, Xavier; Tackley, Paul J. (12 July 2022). "Hadean/Eoarchean tectonics and mantle mixing induced by impacts: a three-dimensional study". Progress in Earth and Planetary Science. 9 (1): 38.

Pavlov, A. A.; Kasting, J. F. (5 July 2004). "Mass-Independent Fractionation of Sulfur Isotopes in Archean Sediments: Strong Evidence for an Anoxic Archean Atmosphere". Astrobiology. 2 (1): 27–41.

Proterozoic Eon

Fakhraee, Mojtaba; Tarhan, Lidya G.; Reinhard, Christopher T.; Crowe, Sean A.; Lyons, Timothy W.; Planavsky, Noah J. (May 2023). "Earth's surface oxygenation and the rise of eukaryotic life: Relationships to the Lomagundi positive carbon isotope excursion revisited". Earth-Science Reviews. 240

Phanerozoic Eon

Glaessner, Martin F. (1961). "Precambrian Animals". Scientific American. 204 (3): 72–78.

Paleo Analysis. (2023, February 22). The complete history of the earth: The great dying. YouTube. https://www.youtube.com/watch?v=x7YKfmRrwHo&t=847s

Wikimedia Foundation. (2024b, April 27). Cenozoic. Wikipedia. https://en.wikipedia.org/wiki/Cenozoic

Cambrian Period

Brett, C. E.; Allison, P. A.; Desantis, M. K.; Liddell, W. D.; Kramer, A. (2009). "Sequence stratigraphy, cyclic facies, and lagerstätten in the Middle Cambrian Wheeler and Marjum Formations, Great Basin, Utah". Palaeogeography, Palaeoclimatology, Palaeoecology. 277 (1–2): 9–33.

Briggs, D. E. G.; Erwin, D. H.; Collier, F. J. (1995), Fossils of the Burgess Shale, Washington: Smithsonian Inst Press, ISBN 1-56098-659-X, OCLC 231793738

"Charles Walcott". Royal Ontario Museum. Archived from the original on 6 June 2013. Retrieved 12 April 2024.

Cambrian Period (cont.)

Fortey, Richard Alan (6 November 1989). "There are extinctions and extinctions: examples from the Lower Palaeozoic". Philosophical Transactions of the Royal Society B: Biological Sciences. 325 (1228): 327–355. Bibcode:1989RSPTB.325..327F. doi:10.1098/rstb.1989.0092. Retrieved 12 April 2024.

Powell, C.M.; Dalziel, I.W.D.; Li, Z.X.; McElhinny, M.W. (1995). "Did Pannotia, the latest Neoproterozoic southern supercontinent, really exist". Eos, Transactions, American Geophysical Union. 76: 46–72.

Smith, Alan G. (2009). "Neoproterozoic timescales and stratigraphy". Geological Society, London, Special Publications. 326 (1): 27–54.

Ordovician Period

Charles Lapworth (1879) "On the Tripartite Classification of the Lower Palaeozoic Rocks", Geological Magazine, new series, 1-15.

M. Marcilly, Chloé; Maffre, Pierre; Le Hir, Guillaume; Pohl, Alexandre; Fluteau, Frédéric; Goddéris, Yves; Donnadieu, Yannick; H. Heimdal, Thea; Torsvik, Trond H. (15 September 2022). 594.

"New type of meteorite linked to ancient asteroid collision". Science Daily. 15 June 2016.

Silurian Period

Brookfield, M. E.; Catlos, E. J.; Suarez, S. E. (2021-10-03). "Myriapod divergence times differ between molecular clock and fossil evidence: U/Pb zircon ages of the earliest fossil millipede-bearing sediments and their significance". Historical Biology. 33.

Nealon, T.; Williams, D. Michael (30 April 2007). "Storm-influenced shelf deposits from the silurian of Western Ireland: A reinterpretation of deep basin sediments". Geological Journal. 23 (4): 311–320.

Devonian Period

Becker, R. T.; Marshall, J. E. A.; Da Silva, A. -C.; Agterberg, F. P.; Gradstein, F. M.; Ogg, J. G. (1 January 2020), Gradstein, Felix M.; Ogg, James G.; Schmitz, Mark D.; Ogg, Gabi M. (eds.), "Chapter 22 - The Devonian Period", Geologic Time Scale 2020, Elsevier, pp. 733–810.

McGhee, George R. (2013). When the invasion of land failed: The legacy of the Devonian extinctions. New York: Columbia University Press.

Carboniferous Period

Sahney, S.; Benton, M.J. & Falcon-Lang, H.J. (2010). "Rainforest collapse triggered Pennsylvanian tetrapod diversification in Euramerica". Geology. 38 (12): 1079–1082.

Scotese, Christopher R.; Song, Haijun; Mills, Benjamin J. W.; van der Meer, Douwe G. (2021-04-01). "Phanerozoic paleotemperatures: The earth's changing climate during the last 540 million years". Earth-Science Reviews. 215.

Permian Period

Andrew Alden. "The Great Permian-Triassic Extinction". About.com Education. Archived from the original on 2012-11-18.

GeoKansas--Geotopics--Mass Extinctions". ku.edu. Archived from the original on 2012-09-20.

Olroyd, D.R. (2005). "Famous Geologists: Murchison". In Selley, R.C.; Cocks, L.R.M.; Plimer, I.R. (eds.). Encyclopedia of Geology, volume 2. Amsterdam: Elsevier. p. 213.

Parrish, J. T. (1995). "Geologic Evidence of Permian Climate". The Permian of Northern Pangea. pp. 53–61.

Triassic Period

Friedrich von Alberti, Beitrag zu einer Monographie des bunten Sandsteins, Muschelkalks und Keupers, und die Verbindung dieser Gebilde zu einer Formation [Contribution to a monograph on the colored sandstone, shell limestone and mudstone, and the joining of these structures into one formation] (Stuttgart and Tübingen, (Germany): J. G. Cotta, 1834). Alberti coined the term "Trias" 324.

Marzoli et al., 1999, Science 284. Extensive 200-million-year-old continental flood basalts of the Central Atlantic Magmatic Province, pp. 618–620.

Jurassic Period

Hosseinpour, Maral; Williams, Simon; Seton, Maria; Barnett-Moore, Nicholas; Müller, R. Dietmar (2016-10-02). "Tectonic evolution of Western Tethys from Jurassic to present day: coupling geological and geophysical data with seismic tomography models". International Geology Review. 58 (13): 1616–1645.

Iturralde-Vinent, Manuel A. (2003-01-01). "The Conflicting Paleontologic versus Stratigraphic Record of the Formation of the Caribbean Seaway". The Circum-Gulf of Mexico and the Caribbean: Hydrocarbon Habitats, Basin Formation and Plate Tectonics. Vol. 79.

Sellwood, Bruce W.; Valdes, Paul J. (2008). "Jurassic climates". Proceedings of the Geologists' Association. 119 (1): 5–17.

Jurassic Period (cont.)

Tennant, Jonathan P.; Mannion, Philip D.; Upchurch, Paul (2016-09-02). "Sea level regulated tetrapod diversity dynamics through the Jurassic/Cretaceous interval". Nature Communications. 7 (1): 12737.

Cretaceous Period

Kazlev, M.Alan. "Palaeos Mesozoic: Cretaceous: The Berriasian Age". Palaeos.com. Archived from the original on 20 December 2010. Retrieved 18 October 2017.

Schulte, P.; Alegret, L.; Arenillas, I.; et al. (2010). "The Chicxulub Asteroid Impact and Mass Extinction at the Cretaceous-Paleogene Boundary" (PDF). Science. 327 (5970): 1214–1218.

Paleogene Period

Scotese, Christopher Robert; Song, Haijun; Mills, Benjamin J.W.; van der Meer, Douwe G. (April 2021). "Phanerozoic paleotemperatures: The earth's changing climate during the last 540 million years". Earth-Science Reviews. 215: 103503.

Steinthorsdottir, M.; Coxall, H. K.; de Boer, A. M.; Huber, M.; Barbolini, N.; Bradshaw, C. D.; Burls, N. J.; Feakins, S. J.; Gasson, E.; Henderiks, J.; Holbourn, A. E.; Kiel, S.; Kohn, M. J.; Knorr, G.; Kürschner, W. M. (23 December 2020). "The Miocene: The Future of the Past". Paleoceanography and Paleoclimatology. 36

Neogene Period

Scotese, Christopher R.; Song, Haijun; Mills, Benjamin J.W.; van der Meer, Douwe G. (April 2021). "Phanerozoic paleotemperatures: The earth's changing climate during the last 540 million years". Earth-Science Reviews. 215: 103503.

Spoor, Fred; Gunz, Philipp; Neubauer, Simon; Stelzer, Stefanie; Scott, Nadia; Kwekason, Amandus; Dean, M. Christopher (March 2015). "Reconstructed Homo habilis type OH 7 suggests deep-rooted species diversity in early Homo". Nature. 519 (7541): 83–86.

Quaternary Period

Wikimedia Foundation. (2024b, April 13). Quaternary. Wikipedia. https://en.wikipedia.org/wiki/Quaternary

Paleocene Epoch

Williams, C. J.; LePage, B. A.; Johnson, A. H.; Vann, D. R. (2009). "Structure, Biomass, and Productivity of a Late Paleocene Arctic Forest". Proceedings of the Academy of Natural Sciences of Philadelphia. 158 (1): 107–127.

Eocene Epoch

Wikimedia Foundation. (2024c, April 22). Eocene. Wikipedia. https://en.wikipedia.org/wiki/Eocene

Oligocene Epoch

Haines, Tim; Walking with Beasts: A Prehistoric Safari, (New York: Dorling Kindersley Publishing, Inc., 1999)

Lyell, Charles (1833). Principles of Geology, ... Vol. 3. London, England: John Murray. p. 54.

Miocene Epoch

Yirka, Bob (August 15, 2012). "New genetic data shows humans and great apes diverged earlier than thought"

Pliocene Epoch

Charles A. Repenning, Richard H. Tedford (2013). Fossils of the Carpathian Region. Indiana University Press. p. 373.

Fauquette, Séverine; Bertini, Adele (28 June 2008). "Quantification of the northern Italy Pliocene climate from pollen data: evidence for a very peculiar climate pattern". Boreas. 32 (2): 361–369.

Pleistocene Epoch

Wikimedia Foundation. (2024, April 9). Pleistocene. Wikipedia. https://en.wikipedia.org/wiki/Pleistocene

Holocene Epoch

Wikimedia Foundation. (2024, May 3). Holocene. Wikipedia. https://en.wikipedia.org/wiki/Holocene

INDEX

Made in the USA
Columbia, SC
21 November 2024

47189861R00108